When visiting

LETCHWORTH . HITCHIN
BALDOCK OR AMPTHILL

Don't forget to call at

NOTT'S CAFÈS

. For your LUNCH or TEA .

Excellent Service   . . . . .   Moderate Prices

WILLOW CAFE
LETCHWORTH

—

EASTCHEAP
RESTAURANT
LETCHWORTH

BRAND ST
HITCHIN

—

HIGH STREET
BALDOCK

—

CHURCH ST.
AMPTHILL

NOTT'S Catering Department are pre-
pared to quote for Dinners, Lunches,
Teas, Banquets, etc. . . Prices Moderate
Service Excellent.

NOTT'S have a reputation for supplying
everything of the best only.   .   .   .

GIVE NOTT'S A TRIAL!

HITCHIN
A Pictorial History

CRICKET MATCH.

Come all ye jovial Hitchiners,
Whose hearts beat high with glee,
Come, see a jolly Cricket Match,
Which long you've wished to see.

A MATCH WILL BE PLAYED

On WEDNESDAY, August 18th, 1869,

BETWEEN THE

HERTFORDSHIRE STRAGGLERS

AND THE

HITCHIN INDEPENDENTS,

IN

Seaman's Close, Gaping Hills,

HITCHIN.

The Stumps will be pitched at Eleven o'clock, and the players will appear in Full Costume, at Half-past; the Hertfordshire Stragglers in their free-and-easy Uniforms and the Hitchin Independents as they like, of course.

On this occasion one of the celebrated greased-lightning Cricket Balls, and Dark's Weeping Willow Bats (supplied by the renowned Mathews) will be used, and the Wickets will be formed of the Wooden Legs of a few old trumps, who will appear on the ground without them. The Umpires will be chosen from the oldest and wisest of cricket veterans, and a professional Scorer has been engaged.

ADMISSION TO THE GROUND:—Respectable looking Pedestrians Threepence each, which amount will be returned to them in refreshments, either liquid or solid.

☞ *The Public are respectfully reminded, that from the circumstance of the ground selected for this match being situated upon an eminence, splendid views may be obtained of the surrounding scenery, interspersed with landmarks of importance—such as Wombwell's Mill, with its sails making rapid revolutions (if there is a strong wind), the Parochial Hostelry with its brick surroundings, the Baronial Hall on Mount Pleasant, the newly-gilded Weather Cock on St. Mary's (which is now ever engaged in pointing out to the way-farer the way the wind blows), and many other objects equally interesting will present themselves, so that an agreeable afternoon may be spent by those who are not great admirers of the manly game of cricket, but who enjoy a day out.*

HITCHIN
A Pictorial History

Richard Field

Phillimore

1991

Published by
PHILLIMORE & CO. LTD.
Shopwyke Hall, Chichester, Sussex

ISBN 0 85033 794 1

Printed and bound in Great Britain by
BIDDLES LTD.,
Guildford, Surrey

*This book is dedicated jointly to my parents for lots of good things,
and to Frances Wilson, a gifted teacher and an inspiration to many*

List of Illustrations

Frontispiece: Cricket match notice, 1869

Acknowledgements

Many thanks to the following for the loan of photographs and postcards and permission to reproduce them here:

Bancroft Players, 164-5; T. Brooker & Sons Ltd., 152-3; Mrs. G. W. Carling, 23, 60, 66, 92; Mr. Andrew Carmichael, 20; Mrs. N. Coxall, 175; Dick Dolan, 79; Priscilla Douglas, 62; Mr. and Mrs. Farey, 170; Foreman-Laws, Frontispiece; Pat Gadd, 9, 16, 34, 73, 88, 90-1, 93-9; Mr. A. W. Gentle, 32, 61, 65; The Mistress and Fellows of Girton College, Cambridge, 115; Mrs. M. Grant, 114; Holy Saviour church, Hitchin, 100-1, 103; Mr. P. Hankin, 14, 21, 24, 30, 35, 58, 78, 82, 106, 112; R. Harkness and Co., 80, 129-32; Hawkins Clothiers Ltd., 154; William Heaton, 2, 19, 29, 36, 37, 59, 63, 69, 83, 109, 171; the Church of Mary Immaculate and St Andrew, Hitchin, 110; Hitchin Museum, 1, 10, 17, 27, 28, 40, 43, 48, 49, 53, 55-7, 67, 70, 74-7, 81, 85, 102, 105, 113, 116-7, 133-4, 136-9, 146-7, 156, 160-1; Francis Newton Ltd., 72, 87, 140-4, 162; Hitchin Thespians, 163; Hitchin Youth Trust (formerly Hitchin Youth Association Ltd.), 39; Norman Hyde Esq., 12, 54, 173-4; Don Kirby, 167-9; Terry Knight, 3-5, 6-8, 13, 15, 18, 22, 25-6, 31, 33, 38, 41-2, 45, 50-2, 68, 71, 84, 89, 107, 111, 135, 150-1, 155, 158, 159; William Ransom & Son plc, 119-123; Mrs. Penny Rogers, 44, 46-7, 158, 166; Mr. P. Russell, 124-8; Mr. R. Sanders; 148-9; Mr. Frank Symons, 145; Mr. Wheeler, 172; Mrs. Ellen Winters, 11, 104. Nos. 54 & 80 are reproduced by courtesy of the *Luton News*, 39 by courtesy of the *North Herts Gazette* and 19 & 30-1, by courtesy of Francis Frith & Co. Ltd. Nos. 11, 91 & 93-4 are reproduced by permission of the Hitchin Museum. The Victorian Chemist Shop at the Hitchin Museum (118) was photographed by courtesy of the Hertfordshire Medical and Pharmaceutical Museum Trust. Thanks to Tony Court of Photone Pictures for prints of the Hitchin Museum photographs listed above and for original photographs 64, 108, 118, 157; and to Derek George Photography for prints of 12 and 154.

Thanks are also due to Mrs. G. W. Carling, Mrs. N. Coxall, Mr. and Mrs. Farey, Mrs. M. Grant, Mr. Frank Symons, Mrs. E. Winter, and Mr. Worboys for their recollections of Hitchin; to Norman Hyde Esq., who suggested ideas that have found their way into this book; to Alison Taylor, acting curator of the Hitchin Museum and her staff who lightened my task with their resourcefulness and unfailing good humour; to Pat Gadd who generously lent me the results of her research on the pubs and inns of Hitchin; to the Reverend David Hall and to Audrey Stewart who gave their time and made available to me information on the history of St Saviour's church; to Father Robert Henshaw for dealing kindly with a fraught and inexperienced writer; to Niki Cross for practical help; and to Terry Knight who read the manuscript and made many useful suggestions. My research has been made immeasurably easier by the work of other writers and researchers, especially Alan Fleck, Nigel Agar, the late Tony Foster, Dick Dolan, Pat Gadd, Victoria Glendinning, Robert Walmsley, Sally Festing and Laslo Grof. There are many others also who have helped with information, photographic material and a great deal of supportive enthusiasm; all of which I gratefully acknowledge. Finally, I would like to thank my partner and friend Diane Shepherd, without whose help, encouragement and forbearance this book would never have been written.

Introduction

This book does not attempt to give a comprehensive account of Hitchin's history: such an undertaking, in the wake of writers like Reginald Hine or Anthony Foster would be a daunting task indeed. Instead, it attempts to capture just a few moments from the town's past, to take a look at the very different kinds of lives that were once lived in familiar streets, and to see what has been saved and what abandoned. Fortunately, the camera arrived in time to record the greatest period of change in Hitchin's history. From 1850 to the present the town has grown from a small but energetic rural community to a sprawling dormitory town. During the same period it has declined in importance: no longer a market centre for livestock, wheat or wool it is nudged on the north and south by new industrial neighbours. However, at the centre of its spreading estates there beats an old but still lively heart. On market days the town centre bustles with shoppers from nearby villages and towns, and rings with a medley of local accents. Its cafés and restaurants buzz with lunchtime conversations over meals that were once served in the local inns. Despite the desire of the '60s for all things new there is sufficient of the old town left to create a strong sense of history, giving life and reality to the written fragments that have come down to us from the past. It is nevertheless true that the town now faces a critical decision; whether to plan for a future of large multiple stores or to go the traditional way, and encourage small specialist shops and businesses.

Expansion

Until the middle of the last century Hitchin remained a compact town, tiny by today's standards, yet still the second largest settlement in the county after St Albans. Its growth over the centuries was slow, and easily contained within a ring of low-lying hills. Situated on the intersection of two important routes, the town showed a simple 'T'-shaped development with Tilehouse/Bridge Street running east and west and Bancroft, north and south. Queen Street, running parallel to Bancroft, was the only significant addition to this plan.

By 1800, however, traditional patterns of life were beginning to change; parliamentary enclosures and the new manufacturing system had already begun to drive people from rural settlements and into the suddenly expanding towns. In Hitchin as elsewhere, tenant farmers, fearful of their future security on the land, were beginning to apprentice their sons to local tradesmen. At the same time displaced farmworkers and their families were making their way into the larger centres seeking work or, in desperate cases, hoping for access to the meagre relief offered by the local 'Guardians of the Poor'. These 'surplus' populations were often driven from their home villages by powerful landowners unwilling to meet the expense of supporting them on the poor rate. In 50 years Hitchin's population more than doubled and by mid-century one in six of the town's population was destitute. New legislation was introduced and Hitchin became the centre of a 'Union' of local parishes organised for the administration of the Poor Law. In 1836, to meet a worsening situation, an enlarged workhouse (now the Hitchin Hospital) was built near Calkdell Farm, just off the Bedford Road.

Despite this sudden influx the town showed little inclination to extend its boundaries. New houses were crammed into existing streets and the number of occupants per household rose. As always the worst effects of this overcrowding fell upon the poor. A government report by William Ranger in 1849 tells of up to 10 people sharing two dingy rooms, perhaps with a single window for light and ventilation, perhaps with none. Sanitary arrangements as we know them today were almost non-existent. Dirt, excrement and offal from slaughterhouses lay everywhere, so it is no surprise to find that in 1848 there were 10,000 attendances at the Hitchin Infirmary alone, and that the health of the population was poor. Even the wealthy often had to put up with the inconvenience of bed bugs and unpleasant smells.

A new and important phase in Hitchin's development began with the arrival of the Great Northern railway in 1850. With this new means of transport and communication came both fresh employment and a new kind of resident: the first London commuters. These were often wealthy men with business in the City, looking for a better quality of life outside the capital. Between the station and the town, a mile distant, houses began to line substantial streets that were previously little more than trackways across open fields. Walsworth Road, Highbury, and The Avenue became the homes of the wealthy and the well-to-do. Radcliffe and Dacre Roads in the same area were cut across cornland and laid out with rows of narrow-fronted terraced houses for railway workers. The town grew, prospered and slowly changed. Yet still, in many ways, it was a coherent community. Hitchin was still small enough for people to know one another, at least by sight, and its newspapers gossiped cosily of the town and its inhabitants, taking local knowledge very much for granted.

The 20th century dawned and the pressure to build became increasingly acute. Bearton Green gave up its name to a group of residential streets and disappeared under bricks and mortar. In the east the town pushed up over the low hills along the Whitehill and Stevenage roads, sweeping across allotments and fields and spilling down the further slope towards the neighbouring villages of Wymondley and St Ipollyts. New estates appeared in the north and south – homes for the Queen Street community displaced in the slum clearances of the 1920s, while to the west rows of houses began to ease their way out through a gap in the encircling hills towards Oughton Head and Ickleford.

It was a difficult and often painful period. Traditional forms of local government appropriate to a world of small craftsmen and country squires became inadequate and had to be reinvented. Large scale planning was now required. A serious outbreak of cholera in Hitchin in 1833 and again in 1848 shocked its inhabitants into action. Taking advantage of new legislation the town elected to set up a Board of Health: its object was to provide Hitchin with its first proper sewage facilities and piped water supply. An engineer was called in.

By the middle of 1852 the work was complete, though at a cost considerably in excess of the original estimates. The board was worried, and with good reason. The pumping engine gave continuous trouble, storm waters backed up into the sewers, pipes leaked, and the deodorising tanks on the edge of town were next to useless. Beset by engineering blunders, mounting debts caused by its own inept management, and threatened by litigation for fouling the river, the Board of Health finally collapsed in 1858 and the receivers were called in. For 15 years the town reverted unofficially to the 'Vestry', a traditional association of ratepayers, in order to run its affairs as best it could, until in 1873 a second Board was created. This was considerably more successful than its predecessor and ran the town until the Hitchin Urban District Council came into being in 1894.

The Markets

The origins of Hitchin Market are now obscure, but it seems that by the middle of the 13th century folk were gathering here regularly to conduct their business. The town's first traders, we may suppose, set up their temporary stalls in a broad, mile-long main street lined with farm houses and cottages. In the course of time more permanent structures appeared and later solidly-built shops. Thus the great width of the medieval street, running the length of Bancroft and on down to the Priory, became filled at its southern end with a jumble of buildings. Between Moss's Corner and Tilehouse Street the Market Place is the sole survivor of a once much larger open space.

Sheep, cattle, corn, vegetables and other goods were brought to market both from local producers and from further afield. Wool was an important commodity in the Middle Ages and the town had a thriving export trade through the 'Staple', a market established at Calais by royal authority in which certain merchants held exclusive trading rights. A number of these merchants were resident in and around Hitchin. Their considerable wealth was almost certainly responsible for the rebuilding of the parish church in the 15th century, for they have left their 'Staple marks' carved upon its walls.

From medieval times the town also excelled in the quantity and quality of its corn. The importance of this trade led in 1853 to the building of the Corn Exchange, an enterprise that owed much of its success to the town's new railway links with London and the North. Soon merchants from as far away as Liverpool were travelling to the town with relative ease and taking up their stands in the new building.

Nearby, the livestock market was being held weekly on its traditional site in Bancroft. But already by the middle of the 19th century it had begun to be a nuisance. Not only was it 'unclean, nauseating and dangerous' but the stock pens erected in the open street obstructed the traffic, creating problems for traders and townsfolk alike. From this time several attempts were made to remove the market to a more convenient site. Plans were drawn up in the early 1850s, and in 1852 a sale notice for the *Horse and Jockey* pub in Old Park Road was advertising the property as being 'near to the proposed cattle market'. No further action was taken, however, and the market stayed where it was. In 1883 frustrated dealers and farmers wrote to the local Board complaining that 'The number of sheep sent to Hitchin on Tuesdays has been on the increase for some years, but the space for penning and showing them to buyers has been much decreased and interfered with by the opening of the New Road to the station'. The 'new road' referred to was Hermitage Road cut through private land in 1874. The local Board considered the complaint but acceded to the wishes of the ratepayers, who objected to a move on the grounds of expense.

In 1902 the Board of Agriculture forced the town's hand by ordering that the Bancroft Market should be closed 'unless the market street is properly paved or a new site is provided'. The recently formed Hitchin Urban District Council sought and obtained a postponement of the closure while it considered the matter. Eventually, one and a half acres of land between Old Park Road and West Lane (now Paynes Park) were leased from the Masters and Fellows of Trinity College, Cambridge, for a period of 99 years. The establishment of the stock market on the new site cost the modest sum of £2,000 and the ratepayers were well pleased.

Meanwhile, the general market continued to flourish in the Market Place. It was a lively and noisy affair, playing host to a wide range of traders, from local grocers to London cheapjack merchants. Those old enough to remember it tell vivid tales of incidents and of characters. There was James Rennie, an Australian-born preacher and bible seller; the Day brothers, with their stock of chamber pots and china ware; John

Pigg, the Royston nurseryman; and a vendor of song sheets who sat at an upright piano playing all the popular tunes of the day. On the Churchgate side of the Square sweet sticky smells of nut brittle and cough candy trickled into the nostrils from the well-known stall of Messrs. Garrett and Cannon.

The central carriageway running from High Street to Sun street was a troublesome affair for shoppers and nervous drivers alike: one old Hitchin resident recalls people crushing themselves under the stalls as he tried to drive a pony and cart through the crowd. Others remember how, as children, on winter evenings, the square seemed a strange and exciting place filled with the hiss of naphthalene flares, and with the soft light and thick shadows they cast over the noisy stalls. But the market was more than just a place for trading or getting in the weekly shopping; it was also an important social event. Pubs and inns around the Square kept extended opening hours, and many who came for the trading would stay to enjoy good basic food and copious quantities of ale at the *Swan* or the *Sun* inns.

Until the turn of the century the south-west corner of the market, near the entrance to Bucklersbury, was given over to the buying and selling of straw plait. Plait markets were strictly regulated and at Hitchin a properly uniformed bellringer was appointed to signal the start of trading as the clock on St Mary's church tower struck nine. But a sharp deal is a sharp deal and illegitimate agreements continued to be struck beforehand by a well-developed system of signals.

The market continued on its traditional site until the outbreak of war in 1939, when it was moved, first to St Mary's Square and then later to its present location south of the churchyard.

The Fire Brigade

In the year 1666, Hitchin's startled inhabitants observed a crimson glow spreading across the town's southern horizon. Messengers on horseback arrived from London and six soldiers from the town were hurriedly despatched with pickaxes and spades. There is no record of their return. The great fire which had fed on thousands of timber-framed buildings in the capital prompted new legislation. Henceforward, churchwardens were responsible for providing their communities with 'Engines, firecocks and leather pipes' to combat the ever-present threat to their combustible towns.

In Hitchin the wardens purchased a small Newsham fire engine to supplement their meagre firefighting equipment of a few hooks and leather buckets. The engine consisted simply of an oak cistern with a brass hand pump in the centre. This machine had a busy life for fires were frequent. In those days firefighting was a haphazard and disorderly affair. The engine was manned by volunteers who, it seems, came more to enjoy the carnival atmosphere and the cheese and ale provided at the expense of the parish than for any other reason. When, on occasion, the expected refreshment failed to arrive, volunteers were nowhere to be found. The engine was an unwieldy affair; it ran on solid wheels, and because it had no means of steering had to be levered round corners. It was kept in the church tower with other firefighting equipment, and since the tower was kept locked there were costly delays. In 1722 two more engines were purchased at a total cost of £22 and the old one was sold, finishing its days quietly as a water trough in the cattle market.

In 1814 a churchwarden named Robert Newton, a builder by trade, suggested that the engines should be transferred to his works yard in Tilehouse street. A committee was formed of prominent townspeople and representatives of insurance agents. Newton's son,

Isaac, was appointed 'Superintendent' of the new brigade together with 24 hand picked 'brigadiers'. Two of Newton's plumbers were henceforth to attend on the engines at each call out to effect any necessary repairs. Isaac proved an able administrator: he mapped the town for suitable water sources and access points, and began the process of moulding the brigade into an effective firefighting force. No doubt civic responsibility was mixed with a shrewd business sense, as the Newtons' building firm must have benefited from the work that grateful property owners put their way.

A succession of superintendents followed. The engines were moved to the Great Yard which ran down to the river from the side of the *Rose and Crown*. Under Isaac Chalkley, a popular man and a strict disciplinarian, a uniform of brass helmets and long tunics was introduced, so that the brigade began to look like proper firemen. It was during Chalkley's time as Captain, as the brigade chief was now called, that the service acquired its first steam-powered pump, a Shand Mason engine that was christened 'St George'. It was noted by more than one observer how arson attacks had suddenly ceased, now that volunteers were no longer needed to man the pumps.

In 1904 a purpose-built fire station was erected at Paynes Park on land that had been leased for the new cattle market. The £711 required was raised by public subscription and organised by Edwin Logsdon, who perhaps more than anyone else was responsible for moulding the Hitchin brigade into an organisation whose skill and efficiency was much admired by other fire establishments. During the First World War the offer of a Mercedes car with a 45 h.p. engine for use as a tractor unit for the steam engine was accepted, and the Mercedes modified to brigade requirements. A second steam engine was bought in 1918, but was replaced six years later by a Morris-Guy petrol engine. In 1941 a National Fire Service was formed to deal with the threat of aerial attack. During the Second World War over 100 high-explosive bombs as well as oil bombs and incendiaries fell on the town, keeping the local fire services busy. Hitchin fire brigade continued to serve the town until 1948 when, despite the wishes of the Urban District Council, a County Service was formed.

Straw Plait

Despite an increasing population throughout the 19th and 20th centuries, Hitchin's hoped-for industrialisation failed to happen. Worried voices were heard in the press and in the council chamber. Hitchin's trade remained founded for the most part on small family businesses, a few of which were to gain a wide, sometimes an international, reputation for excellence but which were never destined to become mass employers of labour. It was in nearby Letchworth, founded in 1903, and not in Hitchin that many townsfolk were to find work: gradually one carriage after another was added to the worker's train bound for the Garden City on weekday mornings.

Straw plait was, apart from agriculture, the one extensive industry that the town produced, but by the last years of the 19th century it was already dead. Not being easily adapted to large-scale mechanisation and therefore to the factory system, it remained a cottage industry to the end. For the poorer sections of the community, however, it was of great importance.

The earliest reference to the making of straw hats in England occurs in 1630 when a number of Hitchin paupers were sent to one Jeremiah Hockley at Ware near Hertford, 'to work at flax dressing, the spinning of linen threads and the making of straw hats'. Fifty years later the towns of Luton and Dunstable in Bedfordshire were emerging as the focus for a growing industry, and by the middle of the 18th century Hitchin had been drawn into their orbit. The town became a market centre for straw plait and a collecting point for the Bedfordshire hat-makers.

The plait produced was at first very coarse, being made usually from the whole 'pipe' of straw. Sometimes the straw was split along its length roughly with a knife to produce work of a somewhat better quality, but it was not until the invention of the 'splitter', a simple device that allowed the straw to be divided evenly into a number of 'splints', that a finer grade plait could be produced.

A dealer would first buy straw directly from the farmer, then, after combing it to remove the haulm, he would make it up into bundles. These were then bleached and sometimes dyed. The straw was sorted by means of sieves and bound in small quantities ready for sale to the plaiters. Most of the straw dealing in Hitchin was done in the Market Square, though from 1863 a corner of the Corn Exchange was also used. In 1874 a Plait Hall was opened in Hollow Lane as a market, but by this time the trade was already in decline and the hall seems to have been a desperate attempt to give a boost to the failing industry.

The plaiter purchased the straws, split them as required and gathered them into a small bundle under her left arm. By bending her head she could then extract a length with her mouth. Moistening the splints with saliva made them more pliable and, if required, enabled their pithy 'rice' sides to be stuck together. Three basic types of plait were produced: Plain, Pearl and Brilliant. 'Pearl' was the simplest and usually taught to children on first learning the craft. 'Brilliant' plaits using single splints, but with only the 'shiny' face showing required considerable skill and experience to produce. Many variants on these basic types were developed and each region specialised in a particular style. That produced in the Hitchin region was known as 'middle twist'. Completed plaits were then bound up into 'scores' of twenty yards and sold to the dealers.

The making of plait was an occupation carried on almost exclusively by the wives and children of farm workers. In a market town such as Hitchin where people lived by a wide variety of trades and skills this meant that plait-making was concentrated in certain areas. Plaiters were found in large numbers in the yards off Back (now Queen) Street, though not in Back Street itself, in Quakers (now West) Alley, and at Bearton and Highbury. On the other hand in the streets south of the station occupied by railway workers it was almost unknown. Men too would sometimes engage in plait-making, mostly as a temporary occupation during the winter months, or at other times when there was little work to be had in the fields.

Agricultural earnings in most of the straw-plaiting area were below subsistence level, though those in Hitchin were a little higher than the surrounding villages. Additional income was therefore essential if a family was to stay clear of the poor house. Accounts vary of the money to be earned by plaiting straw. During the Napoleonic wars foreign imports of plait from Leghorn in Italy were curtailed and the local markets thrived. Some reports during this period tell of women earning as much as 5s. a day, several times the wage of an agricultural worker. On the other hand in 1867 when the industry was already in its final decline the wage could be as low as 3s. a week.

Plaiting was not only important as an additional source of income for the family as a whole, but it also gave women a degree of independence that those under the eye of a master could not achieve. Plaiters were also able to afford to dress more smartly than those dependent solely on agricultural wages. Unfortunately, this was often to provide a stamping ground for middle-class ignorance: 'Fornication is lamentably frequent ... and having an extreme fondness for dress, they no doubt often resort to prostitution as a means of adding to their scanty earnings'. This remark, betraying a multitude of prejudices by a Hertfordshire vicar, is by no means an isolated example.

It is quite probable that a degree of resentment lay behind much of the pejorative comment. Around the turn of the century Arthur Young wrote, 'There is so much plaiting at Hitchin, that they will not go into service'. It is worth noting also that the one popular ballad about plaiting that has come down to us has a significantly different angle on the subject:

> In Buckinghamshire and Hertfordshire,
> Mind maidens what you're at,
> And shun the naughty married men,
> Who deal in ladies plait.

The industry was a mixed blessing. Plaiters worked for 12 to 14 hours a day, finding time to look after their homes and children as best they could. When the industry was depressed and the price of plait fell, the only recourse was to work through the night as well. The demise of the industry came in the latter part of the 19th century with a huge influx of cheap plait from China and Japan. In Hitchin plaiters struggled on to earn a living hoping for better times but it was a vain hope: in 1911, during the Coronation celebrations of George V, a float representing 'The Old Plaiting Industry' nostalgically signalled the end of a way of life.

Lavender and Other Plants

> At the expiration of their fifth year [the lavender plants] ... are grabbed up and consigned to the flames. This sacrifice is an annual thing, and so begins the bonfires, and so powerful is the aromatic fragrance given thus to the winds, that Hitchin is to its last court and alley for days together a town of sweet smells.

Thus wrote a visitor to the town in the heyday of its lavender industry. Hitchin is no longer 'a town of sweet smells' for the lavender has gone, but for more than 100 years it thrived on the western hillsides, attracting many a curious visitor during the summer months.

The story begins in 1790 when a chemist by the name of Harry Perks established a pharmacy in the town. In 1823 Harry's son laid the foundations of the future industry by planting lavender. By 1840 when Edward's son Samuel succeeded to the business 35 acres in all were under cultivation at Mount Pleasant on the Pirton Road and at Grays Lane and Gaping Hills. The plant is not native to this country and requires special care if it is to thrive here commercially, but there is some quality, perhaps of the climate, perhaps of the soil, that gives English lavender water a degree of perfection that cannot be matched elsewhere. English plants when transported abroad have failed to produce oil of the same high quality.

Perks' lavender was cropped from around the first week in August and bound into 22-pound sheaves. Hand sickles were used right up until 1961 when the rising cost of labour finally brought the business to a close. The women who performed this work were often from families that for several generations sent members to the Hitchin lavender fields. They worked for a meagre 6d. a day and free lemonade. The sheaves were then taken to the Perks' yard behind the shop in High Street where Woolworth's now stands. The stalks were removed and the flowers were then ready for the stills. Bees grown hopelessly drunk on the scent and still clinging to the blooms were a regular hazard of the work.

In Roman times lavender water was made from a simple decoction of the blooms in water. By Perks' day it was the 'essential oil' that was extracted from the plants and then blended with 20 to 40 times its bulk of spirit. Each batch from Perks' 550-gallon still yielded just one pint of the precious oil. Tending the stills required experience and fine judgement. Allowing the fire to continue burning after the oil began to run risked the 'brimming over' of plant material into the collecting vat thus ruining the entire batch. A batch was turned out every four hours and it took Perks' about three weeks to distil the year's harvest. The oil was then bottled and left for four years to mature. Upwards of 2,000 gallons of lavender water were produced annually.

Perks produced a wide range of products beside lavender water: there was a lavender bloom toilet soap, and a lavender charcoal dentifrice advertised by its producer as 'A new preparation that the proprietor believes has never before been introduced to the public': these were the days before the invention of toothpaste. Samuel Perks took over the premises next door to his chemist shop and in 1877 went into partnership with Charles Llewellyn. As 'Perks and Llewellyn' the firm established a national and then an international reputation for its product, winning the Paris Exhibition Prize Medal in 1867 and a similar award in Philadelphia in 1876. Henceforward, it produced only 'Prize Medal lavender water'.

The Perks' enterprise was soon to be followed by others, most notably William Ransom, a chemist, who in 1846 established a business in the preparation not only of lavender but of a wide range of herbal extracts. Cultivated fields of henbane, peppermint, squirting cucumber, deadly nightshade, and a certain variety of rhubarb soon appeared on the edges of the town. The rhubarb was used for the distillation of an emetic, as, it is said, some of the townsfolk learned to their cost. Each year from May onwards local people pushed, carried, and hauled sacks and barrows, handcarts and even aprons full of wild herbs through Ransom's medieval gateway in Bancroft. Dandelion roots, buckthorn, hemlock and many others were paid for by weight. It was not long before a little cunning taught people to pick poppy petals early in the morning when they were still wet with dew and therefore heavier. Some tried adding stones to their loads. In the 1870s up to 40 tons of dandelion roots and 20 tons of hemlock were collected and paid for each year. But the business was by no means restricted to preparing local herbs: from far-flung regions of the globe came exotic plants: buchu leaves from South Africa, benzoin from Sumatra, squills from Italy, rhubarb from China, scammony root from Mexico and, still packed in their monkey skins, bitter aloes, from far-away Socotra.

Hitchin was an ideal choice for William Ransom's 'physic farm', for within the district there are many different soil types suitable for the growing of a wide variety of herbs. The climate is relatively sunny and dry which minimises the winter losses that occur in wetter conditions. The original 70 acres of farmland increased until by the time of the firm's centenary in 1946 it was cultivating over two hundred. Today, the Ransom's farmlands around Hitchin have been sold, and the firm itself is due to move to a larger site in nearby Biggleswade.

Inns and Brewing

With all the fine cornland to the north of Hitchin suitable for growing barley as well as wheat, it was almost inevitable that the town should develop a malt-producing and a brewing industry. By the time of Elizabeth I, Hitchin's malt already had a high reputation for quality. Far more was produced than could be used locally and much of the surplus was sent to London. But there was no shortage of local brewers. Many of their names have come down to us from the 17th century onwards, sometimes in connection with indictments for operating unlicensed brewhouses, but until recent times there are only glimpses, just enough for us to know that they were here.

By the 19th century a fuller picture begins to emerge. Breweries large and small are recorded in Bancroft, Bucklersbury, Sun Street, Portmill Lane, Back Street, Tilehouse Street, Market Place, and even in Radcliffe Road. The *Sun* brewed its own beer for fifty years from at least the middle of the 19th century; the *Peacock* in Queen Street and the *Bedford Arms* did the same. William Lewin, bearer of a good Hitchin name, had a hand in several enterprises. He first appears as occupier of a house and brewery in Silver Street (the northern end of Bancroft). By 1862 he was brewing in Port Mill Lane and advertising 'Superior Home Brewed Ale':

X Ale	at 1s	per gallon
XX Ale	at 1s 2d	per gallon
XXX Ale	at 1s 4d	per gallon

The 'Triangle Brewery' was his next venture, but the enterprise failed within a few years and the property was sold by George Jackson, the auctioneer, for £61 18s. 0d. Lewin's name finally appears as the publican of the *Swan* in the Market Place. Until the mid 1800s there were two breweries in Sun Street. One, owned by the Crabb family, and later by John Marshall and Joseph Margetts Pierson, was forced to close in 1841 when a disastrous overseas venture ruined the two partners. When it was sold the business consisted of '50 inns and pubs, a capital brewhouse, 2 family residences, malthouses, cottages and numerous valuable parcels of land in Sun Street'. The sale achieved high prices despite, as William Lucas put it, 'the spread of teetotalism, and the very bad state of repair and low trade in consequence of the badness of their beer'. Joseph Margetts Pierson, nothing daunted, went on the following year to build another brewing business at the southern end of Bucklersbury. The other brewery in Sun Street was that owned by William Lucas and his brother Samuel. The business was established in 1709 and for six generations there was to be an eldest son named William at the head of the firm. The family were Quakers, a fact which caused at least one William Lucas, the Diarist, to struggle with his conscience over the nature of his business. In 1896 the firm became a limited company. Ten years later, another William was sufficiently vexed by 'extortionate' taxation aimed specifically at brewers to justify his line of business in the local paper. In 1921 the business was sold to the Luton firm of J. W. Green Ltd. and two years later it was closed down.

There can be no doubt that, with the appalling condition of the water supply in Victorian Hitchin, beer was a far safer drink. The Ranger report of 1849 carried out by the Central Board of Health concluded that many of the town's 92 wells were polluted and the river from which people often drew their water was also used as an open sewer. The Lucas brewery at least, which supplied a number of pubs around the town, took great care to use only pure water for beer-making. Alcohol was consumed in. huge quantities in Hitchin. In 1849 over £10,000 was spent on drink in one year alone, and by 1884 there was one pub for every 110 inhabitants, a figure that was exceeded in the county only by Ware. It is not surprising therefore that Hitchin pubs were often rowdy places. Many were forced to close for keeping disorderly houses, and a number of landlords were indicted personally for bad behaviour. In 1870 James Andrews, the tenant of the *Orange Tree* was fined 13s. for being drunk and riotous on Windmill Hill. Having lost its licence the *Trooper* at Moss's corner reopened, first as the *Ram* and then, in an attempt, it seems, to improve its reputation, as the *Reform*. This didn't work, and in 1870 the magistrates closed it down once more.

Besides being places to drink, inns were traditionally expected to provide entertainment. The *Swan* which stood in the corner of the Market Square, on the site of the present Arcade, had its own stage and was noted for theatrical productions. Nearby, at the *Red Lion*, demolished to make way for the Corn Exchange *c.*1852, there was a 2d. waxworks. But the entertainments offered were more often sports, particularly blood sports. Cockfighting was popular and gave its name to the *Cock Inn* in High Street. It is also recorded that the *Red Lion* was the venue for an encounter between 'the Gents. of Hitchin and Cambridge with 14 Cocks a side'. But there were quieter pleasures to be had at the *Sun* and the *Ship* in Walsworth, both of which had excellent bowling greens; and if bowling was not to one's taste there were always billiards, quoits or skittles.

Scale of Chains

1. In the centuries before 1850 there was little change in the layout of Hitchin's streets. Bancroft, the main thoroughfare, had grown up along the line of a major trackway from London to Bedford, while Tilehouse/Bridge Street followed another route connecting two important medieval garrisons at Pirton and Wymondley. By 1818, when this map was drawn, some development had begun along Back and Dead Streets (now Queen Street) and along Tilehouse Street, but there was as yet no indication of the sudden expansion that would take place with the arrival of the railways in 1850.

2. St Mary's, one of the largest parish churches in the country, was built, it seems, by local merchants with little regard to cost. Its early history is an extraordinary catalogue of disasters. The first church on this site was destroyed by fire, and the second by the great wind of 1115. In 1292, rebuilt, it was struck by lightning and badly damaged. Six years later an earthquake hit and caused the central portion to collapse. In 1304 the roof caved in. This photograph of the church's east end dates from the early 1930s.

3. The most photographed view of Hitchin, showing the top of St Mary's low but massive tower with its needle spire. The tower dates from 1190 and is the oldest part of the church. The railings were erected in 1828 following a series of bodysnatching incidents in the churchyard. At the time of this view, *c.*1902, the upper part of the building nearest the church was the studio of H. G. Moulden, photographer and church organist, who left a fine collection of photographs of the town.

4. Hermitage Road, though cut in 1874, remained undeveloped until the late 1920s. Seen here *c.*1922, the old Hermitage house is on the left while across the road are the premises of P. H. Barker and Son, timber merchants. Until 1919 these buildings had been hidden behind a line of ancient box trees planted in the reign of Edward IV and unusual for their great size. The house on the summit of Windmill Hill is the home of John Barker, owner of the timber firm. Later in the decade, as Councillor Barker, he would become a prime mover in the building of St Mary's Square.

5. In this view of Hermitage Road in the 1950s, the Hermitage has given way to a now familiar range of shops. Barker's, having modified its premises in the late '20s, is by this time presenting a Tudor-style frontage to the street. Further up the road another 'Hermitage' has appeared; the short-lived but well-remembered Hermitage Cinema. Built in 1931-2 the Hermitage was one of the best equipped cinemas of its generation. Both Barker's and the cinema would succumb to another spate of rebuilding in the 1960s.

6. Rapid increases in population in the first half of the 19th century led to overcrowding and to the development of slum conditions in the Queen Street area. By mid-century densely-packed houses were crowding up against the river at the eastern end of St Mary's church. The cramped and insanitary yards around which many of these houses clustered contrasted starkly with the elegant Georgian façades just 500 yards away in Bancroft.

7. The Back Street (now Queen Street) yards were crammed into a small area on or close to the site of present day St Mary's Square. In this photograph of Chapman's Yard the houses are no more than the width of a single window and door. Typically, they contained two rooms, less often, three. An official inspection of 1849 records that six of the houses shown here had between seven and 10 occupants each. Open soil pits, often close to the house and rarely emptied because of expense, were all the sanitary arrangements most of the yards' residents had – if they had any at all.

8. It was not until 1921 that much of the Queen Street area was declared insanitary under the 1890 Housing Act. In 1924 work began to clear the slum dwellings: to house displaced residents, A. T. Blood, the council surveyor, drew up plans for the new Sunnyside estate south of the town. In time, the river was re-routed and dammed, and the whole area flattened. In this view, *c*.1928, the open space that was to become St Mary's Square has appeared at the foot of Windmill Hill.

9. Back Street (now Queen Street), *c*.1910. All these buildings have now gone. The *Bricklayers Arms*, which was rebuilt in 1923, a year before the clearances began, survives in name alone. Several of the numerous pubs for which the area was notorious can be seen further up the road. Next door to the *Bricklayers* a small grocer's shop is advertising Moss's tea which was packed by that firm at its warehouse in nearby Portmill Lane.

10.   Queen Street and the top of Portmill Lane, at the end of the last century. On the right, behind the assembled group, is a fence which closes off the slopes of Windmill Hill: at this time the hill formed part of the Hermitage estate.

11.   It would appear by their tidy dress that these children in Queen Street are pupils of the British School which stands behind them in the centre of the photograph. For 500 years after the great plague of 1349 decimated the town's population, this part of Queen Street was known as Dead Street. In later epidemics the street lived up to its fearful name: in 1557 fifty people died and were buried in a pit nearby, while in 1665 not a soul survived.

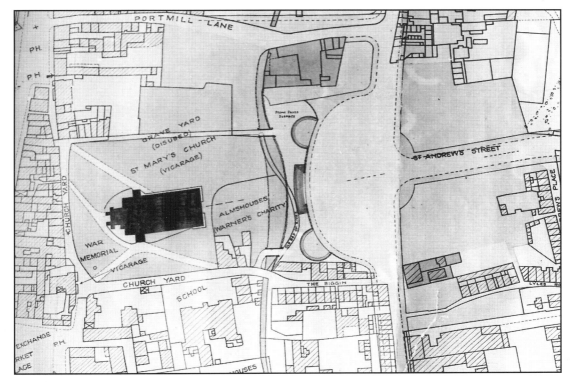

12.   This plan for the development of the Back Street slums is dated 1926, two years after demolition had begun, and signed by A. T. Blood, Surveyor. The plan was less elaborate than that eventually adopted, though the basic idea of a large open space with St Mary's church as a focal point is already evident. The scenic possibilities of the river are not so well developed as in the plans that were eventually adopted.

13.   An architect's drawing of the 1929 St Mary's Square plan by Bennett and Bidwell. The Hitchin Urban District Council accepted the design as far as the open space was concerned but would not commit itself to build the surrounding shops. Ultimately the bordering area was left to piecemeal development with the result that the Square still looks unfinished. It is interesting to speculate whether some of the ancient buildings in the High Street and Bancroft might have been spared had St Mary's Square developed as the main shopping area of the town, as this drawing suggests.

14.   The old jettied buildings in this photograph of The Triangle, at the foot of Hitchin Hill, were purchased by the Council in 1928 for demolition in a road-widening scheme. The scheme was never implemented and the buildings survived for another 30 years, finally giving way to a garage. The cottages in Queen Street on the right have also gone. Lying at the foot of a hill on the main entrance to the town from the south, The Triangle was an early accident blackspot as a 'Drive Slowly' sign on the lamp-post indicates.

15.   The town supported two temperance hotels into the early years of the 20th century, one in Brand Street and the *Triangle Hotel* at the foot of Hitchin Hill. The hotel was also the headquarters of the North London Cycling Club, which met here regularly at weekends. The cycling boom was at its height right into the 1920s when a traffic survey in Nightingale Road counted 8,865 bicycles in one week, as against 2,703 motor cars and 1,694 horse-drawn vehicles.

16. There have been several changes in Bridge Street since this photograph was taken *c.*1910. In 1924 the Lucas Brewery buildings, just beyond the bridge, were sold for £2,275. Thirty-nine years later they were demolished and replaced by Crown House. Gone too are the maltings on the extreme right of the photograph. On the left is the sign of the *Royal Oak*, formerly the *Boot*, which survived until 1922 when its licence was refused, a fate shared by many of the town's pubs.

17. Lying at the foot of Tilehouse Street and Hitchin Hill, and occupied by the usually mild-mannered River Hiz, Bridge Street has always been subject to flooding. On 23 July 1912, in two cloudbursts, the skies delivered an astonishing 3.07 inches of rain. Within minutes the Hiz had burst its banks, storm drains had backed up, basements were awash, and bits of market stall were seen floating down Sun Street. A fascinated *Hertfordshire Express* reporter likened the torrential rain to the 'rapid dither' of the cinematograph – newly arrived at the Picturedrome in Ickleford Road.

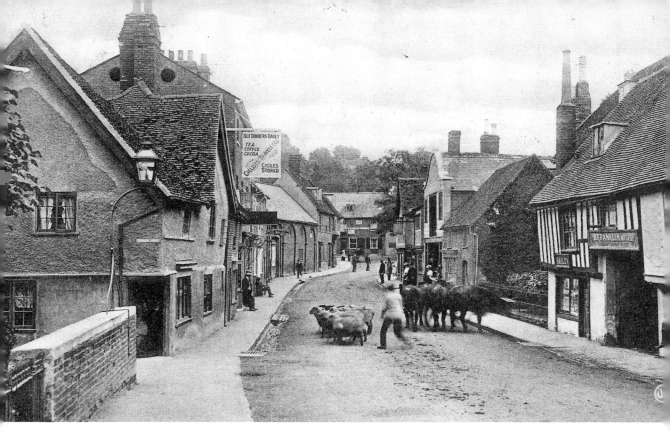

18.   Sheep and cattle were a common sight in the town's streets until the early decades of this century. Bridge and Tilehouse Streets lay on the traditional drovers' route to London and, as well as local livestock, large numbers of Highland cattle were often herded through this part of the town. On the right is a row of attractive 15th-century houses owned, until 1960, by the Radcliffes, as part of the Priory estate. Part of this row was the home of Robert Odell, farrier, whose family occupied several properties in the road.

19.   Bridge Street in the 1960s. The house on the extreme left of the picture has now acquired four curious green and white dragons over its doorway, thought to be the work of Gerard Ceunis, artist and former proprietor of Maison Gerard in the Market Place. The maltings are now just an empty site, but the timbered buildings on the right have managed to survive despite plans to demolish them. Their low-lying position is a legacy from the days when the river was crossed by a ford.

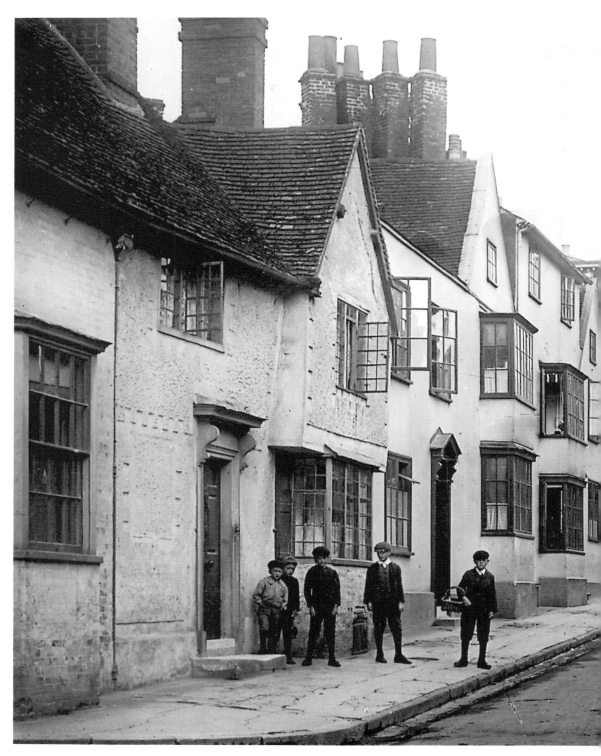

20. Tilehouse Street, here seen around the turn of the century, is one of the town's oldest thoroughfares. By 1970 the traffic problem had become so acute that drastic remedies were required. The old street was sealed off, and a new bypass built to divert traffic from the south via Old Park Road. There are no modern developments in the street. In its now quiet length it is possible to read almost an entire history of English domestic architecture up to the 19th century.

21. Sun Street looking north, *c*.1895. The street has been known both as St Mary's Street and as Angel Street after the old inn at its narrow Market Place end. The 'Angel' of the inn's title was the Angel of the Annunciation. The inn had close connections with the Church, whose Archdeaconry courts were held on its premises until the early 17th century. In later years the Hitchin Fire Brigade met here regularly for its annual dinner. As the neighbouring *Sun Inn* rose in importance so the name of the street changed.

22. Sun Street *c*.1905, looking south from the Market Place. The magnificent plane and sycamore trees that closed off the street by the Priory horsepond have now sadly gone. On the right, high on the wall, is the sign of 'Paternoster, Printers'. This sign still exists as a memorial to a once thriving business. From this building the Paternosters published the *Hitchin Advertiser*, and later Charles Hales and Miss Paternoster ran a lending library and reading rooms as well as a printing works.

23.   Bucklersbury, *c*.1870. In 1869 Charles Hales arrived in Hitchin from London, and bought the premises on the corner of Bucklersbury. Eighteen months later he went into partnership with Miss Sarah Paternoster whose family business had been long established in Sun Street. Surviving its founders the firm of Paternoster and Hales continued to publish all kinds of handbills, election notices and postcards, until quite recent times. Further down the street is the *George*, one of the oldest buildings in the town, but much altered since this photograph was taken.

24. A pawnbroker's sign hung outside 8 Bucklersbury since at least 1890, when Hookham and Son were the proprietors. After 1902 the business was carried on by Fred Morely. Whether trade was good or bad is uncertain but in 1936 the business suddenly changed its name to become Fred Morely and Co. Ltd., and a jeweller's. In this view, *c.*1918, the premises on the left of the photograph are occupied by Charles W. Chew, leather merchant. The building opposite the *George* sign has not yet acquired its curious false gable.

25. The familiar landmarks of Barclays Bank and the Corn Exchange firmly identify this view, *c.*1920, as the High Street leading into the Market Place. Otherwise a great deal has changed. In 1931 two thirds of the *Cock Inn* was demolished to make way for a new Woolworth's store. In 1964 Woolworth's purchased a larger building from Perks and Llewellyn on the other side of the *Cock* which they also demolished, replacing it with a 20th-century pastiche. A branch of Boot's now occupies the old Woolworth's site. The buildings opposite have had their roof line 'tidied up'.

26. This photograph from the mid-1930s shows the now severely truncated *Cock Inn* with Woolworth's 3d. and 6d. Stores established in its place.

27. After the arrival of the railways, local carters continued to run regular road services from Hitchin to nearby villages, calling at some of the town's pubs to pick up items for transportation. Parcels could be left for delivery in the unattended wagons in Brand Street well into the 1920s without any fear of them being stolen. At the top of the photograph it is possible to make out the shape of the windmill, which was destroyed by fire in 1875, on Windmill Hill.

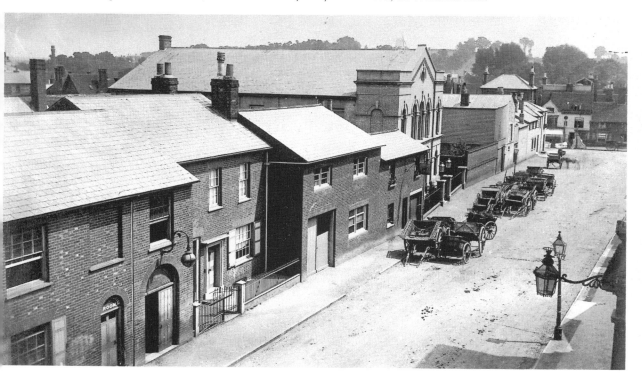

28. Basketwork stands outside the shop of James Bullard in the churchyard, *c*.1908. The Bullard family were basketmakers in Hitchin for several generations, until James' death in 1913. In 1948, work done on the building to the left revealed that the chimney still had its original cow-dung parging, once a common form of flue lining. The house journal of Fosters, the builders responsible for the work, commented that 'this is in good condition and sticks like glue'.

29. The Wesleyan Sunday School, *c*.1904, outside the chapel in Brand Street, now the site of a supermarket. The children are all dressed in their Sunday best for the occasion. The Methodists, a flourishing community at the time this picture was taken, were late to establish themselves in this Quaker-dominated and Non-conformist town. Beyond the chapel is the *Dog Inn*, where cattle drovers and Gypsies met to drink and do business on market days, and further up the street is one of Hitchin's temperance hotels.

30. A view of Bancroft in the 1950s, looking north. Near the corner of Hermitage Road behind the lamp-post are three shops that were to be demolished in 1958 to make way for a Co-Operative retail store. The façade, though 17th-century, was known to conceal an interior at least 200 years older. During demolition it was discovered that the middle two-thirds of the row was a medieval hall house, with the entire roof and main timbers still intact. Unfortunately the Co-Op did not find it possible to incorporate the medieval hall into its design.

31. Bancroft in the 1950s, looking south. On the right is the 'Waters building'. Alfred Waters described himself as an ironmonger, iron and colour dealer, tinware manufacturer and furniture dealer. At his 'Bancroft Stores' in 1914 you could buy a footwarmer, a gas mantle, a garden roller, a 'good and stylish pram' to enhance the effect of a well-turned-out baby, or you could ask to have the contents of your home removed. The Georgian building was demolished in 1967 and the site purchased several years later by Safeways.

32. This view shows a tree-lined and largely residential Bancroft in 1911. The ancient sycamores that stood either side of the Hermitage Road entrance were old and hollow, but survived until one of them was blown across the carriageway in 1915. The other was removed for safety reasons soon after. Further up the road on the right-hand side a house next to the Croft is being rebuilt.

Bancroft, Hitchin

33. By 1879 the Hitchin bridewell, the local jail, now a private house in a corner of Bancroft Recreation Ground, was in a sorry state of repair and for many years there were doubts about its security. It took six years to find a suitable site for the new police station and petty sessions court, but it was eventually built in Bancroft, seen here on the right of the photograph. The building is now used as the magistrates' court.

34. Old Park Road bears much of today's heavy traffic entering the town from Luton and the south. It is hard to imagine it was ever as quiet as in this photograph, taken about 1900. The houses on the western side of the road were some of the first to be built as the town began to expand in the middle of the 19th century, while the land opposite remained meadowland until 1903, when it was leased to the Council for the new cattle market.

35.   The Avenue, with its now stately trees at the sapling stage. Built during the Edwardian era its four-bedroomed houses were home to the well-to-do, their families and their servants. The Nettledell estate, of which The Avenue is part, is built on land formerly excavated as lime pits.

36.   A view of Whinbush Road, looking towards Nightingale Road *c.*1905. The lamplighter was, no doubt, a familiar figure to this little girl, but standing in the gateway of her house she was about to witness new developments that would eventually change her life. Around the time this photograph was taken the Electrical Supply Corporation Ltd. of London had just been granted a lease to build Hitchin's first electricity generating plant almost directly opposite her front door.

37.   The year is 1909, and the children of St Saviour's School are parading along Radcliffe Road on the occasion of their annual Sunday School treat. Fifty years previously a photographer standing on this spot would have captured waving cornfields, and in the distance a rough track that would in later years become Nightingale Road. On the left is the large canopy of the Walsworth Road sub post office. The bell turret of St Saviour's can just be seen above the now vanished trees.

38.   Grove Road was built around the turn of the century on land that had previously been a nursery. There was no road here before that time, just a path leading to Grove Mill on the far side of the railway embankment. The River Hiz, crossed by five little footbridges, also passed over this land. By 1910 the river flowed behind the backs of the houses on the right, and new bridges gave the occupants access to their kitchen gardens. Since the Hiz was prone to flood in this area, the gardens were frequently inundated.

39.   Members of Hitchin Youth Club are setting out from their clubhouse, a former Church Army hut at Woodside, on a brisk spring day in April 1947. Behind them are the massive Victorian façades of the large houses built after the railways arrived in 1850.

40. In recognition of the town's success in raising a large sum of money for the war effort, Hitchin was presented in October 1919 with a tank known in its battle days as 'Fearless'. The tank had seen action in France at the battle of Cambrai with the sixth battalion of the Tank Corps, but was relatively undamaged by the event. Mounted on a concrete plinth at the north end of Butts Close, Fearless remained a familiar sight until, at the outbreak of the Second World War, it was removed, somewhat the worse for wear, and used for scrap.

41.   Parts of Oughton Head were formerly grazed, but today the area is given over to recreation. It was once one of the finest wetland sites in the county and boasted a wide variety of wildlife: the Oughton teemed with trout and stickleback, and kingfishers darted about the river bank. Bitterns and great snipe have been recorded in the marshlands. The water levels have fallen now despite the work of conservationists, and much of the wildlife has gone. Those agile enough to climb the beech trees might still see the initials of lovers carved there before the First World War when this view was taken.

42.   A view of the River Purwell at Walsworth in about 1905, much wider than it is today. Until the coming of the railway, Walsworth was a secluded hamlet a mile and a half from the town; so isolated, that boys could bathe naked in a pool formed by the river near the Woolgrove Road railway bridge without fear of being discovered by anyone except the crews of passing locomotives. A quick duck underwater usually dealt with that.

43. This aerial view of Hitchin town centre dates from about 1957 and shows the blocks of market infill from Tilehouse Street to Moss's Corner. In earlier times this area was a large open space where local merchants came to set up their stalls and trade in the Tuesday market. The infill buildings lying crammed together in a random development may well have property boundaries that remain unchanged since medieval times.

44. Bancroft, seen here in about 1900, was the traditional site of Hitchin's weekly livestock market until 1904. Despite its width, the sheep pens at its southern end interfered with the free flow of traffic. In addition, it was noisy and smelly. Until this century the handsome line of buildings on the west side

of Bancroft were all residential and unspoiled by plate-glass frontages, though the nuisance value of the market to Bancroft residents must have been considerable.

45. Life in a country town could be fraught with hazards when, as in Hitchin, sheep and cattle were driven right into the town centre on market days. There are numerous accounts of people seeking hasty refuge in doorways and even of frightened cattle being ejected from shops. In 1903 the son of the Reverend B. N. Switzer, a curate at St Mary's, was tossed by a cow in Bancroft. In this view of 1902, a group of cattle is standing at the top of Hermitage Road. The gaslamp on the left was the first in the town to be converted to electricity.

46. In 1847 George Jackson, auctioneer and valuer, held his first livestock sale in Hitchin in the *Swan* yard, now The Arcade and nearby car park. In a few years his auctions were being held regularly on Tuesdays to coincide with the market in Bancroft. In 1878 Jackson acquired the *Cock Inn* and set up his cattle sales and site offices in the yard at the back. This photograph shows his saleyard at Paynes Park. The building in the background is Agadir, built by Jonas Kershaw, publican of the *Swan*, and later given to the town by the Moss family for the town's museum and library.

47. Easter lambfall, 1939, at the lairage in Paynes Park. The weekly livestock market thrived on its new site until the late '60s when, with changes in the pattern of trading and restrictive legislation to stop the spread of Foot and Mouth disease, it came to a close. The Town Hall in Brand Street can be seen behind the stock wagons on the right of this photograph.

48. The general market in Hitchin was not just a place to do business or the weekly shopping but was also an important social event. The principal inns served a market ordinary, a good meal at a moderate cost, to attract extra custom. Large quantities of ale were consumed. When this photograph was taken in 1893 a wide variety of goods were regularly on sale in the market, from domestic items to farm implements.

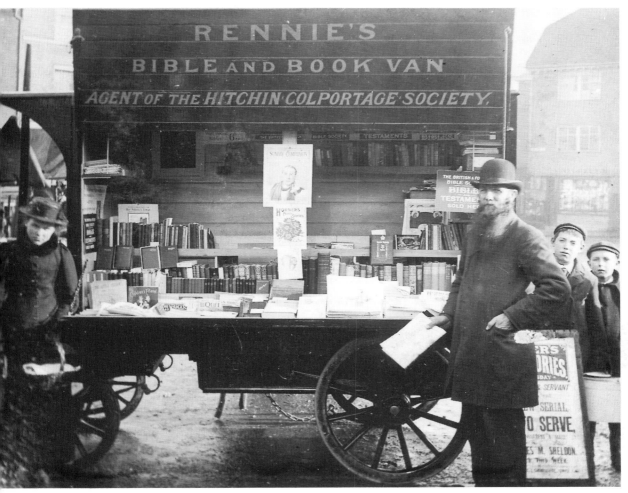

49. James Rennie, an Australian-born Scotsman, was a familiar visitor to Hitchin Market in the early years of this century. He first arrived carrying his religious books and tracts on his back in the old tradition of colportage, but was later provided with a handcart by the Hitchin members of the Baptist and Foreign Bible Society. His evangelism took a practical turn, for he is said to have dug 120 poles of garden ground for poor householders in one year alone.

63164

50. Market day in the Square, c.1905. The restaurant to the right of the Corn Exchange bears the name of Edwin Logsdon over the door. Besides being a restaurant proprietor (1898), Logsdon was also the publican of the *Sun Inn* (1899), and captain of the Hitchin Fire Brigade (1895). It is just possible to make out the post box in front of Briggs' shoe shop on the right of the picture. The box was installed about this time and is a reminder that until 1904 Briggs' shop was the site of the Hitchin Post Office.

51. Summer-time in Edwardian Hitchin. Mr. Brolia, the ice-cream vendor, a familiar figure to the children standing nearby, has set up his stall in the Market Place. Three men appear to be busy on the front of Liptons, one perching rather precariously outside an upper window. The shop windows are empty: perhaps it is 1909 and Liptons is just moving into the premises. On the corner, Freeman Hardy and Willis is selling shoes – as it still does. Its sign is unchanged except for the ornamental pediment which has been removed.

52. Hitchin Market Place, *c.*1924. In 1884 Gatwards, the ironmongers, demolished the *Swan Hotel* and replaced it (centre) with a building designed to harmonise with the Italianate styles of the Corn Exchange and Barclays Bank in High Street. The entrance to the Playhouse has arrived next door to Hobley's restaurant, now with its timbers exposed (see 50), and is advertising 'Perfect Pictures and Refined Variety'. On the other side of Gatwards, Merrick, the confectioner, has now taken over from Black Jack's Cigar Store.

53. At the outbreak of the Second World War, the general market was moved to St Mary's Square in order to make way for a large standing water tank. The tank was one of about thirty water supply points for the use of the fire brigade in the event of bombing raids. As it turned out the Luftwaffe were looking for bigger fish than Hitchin, and the Market Square tank seems to have been used mainly to dampen Saturday night spirits at closing time.

54. War Weapons Week was inaugurated in Hitchin on 12 April 1941 with the aim of encouraging townspeople to lend money to the government, by purchasing a variety of savings certificates and war bonds. The target aimed at was £100,000. At 11 o'clock on the morning of 19 April, Major Guy Kindersley, Chairman of the Hitchin and District War Savings Committee, is seen here setting the figure at £325,000. Higher figures were reported by the end of the week. The stand in the form of a spring balance is secured pragmatically to the Market Place telephone kiosk. In the background the Corn Exchange is advertising roller skating.

55. The Old Town Hall in Brand Street, now council offices, was erected in
1840 by a private company to provide Hitchin with public assembly rooms.
Next door, the subscription library of the Mechanics' Institute, originally
housing 6,000 volumes, was built in 1861 in the same Italianate style. Despite
its grand appearance the old Town Hall was small and badly ventilated.
Towards the end of the century magistrates refused a licence for the
performance of stage plays, because of poor exit arrangements.

56. In 1897 Frederic Seebohm of the Hermitage, and William and Alfred Ransom, offered to donate land on a site opposite
the old Town Hall for the building of new assembly rooms. The Council, who had until this time used rented office space
for their meetings, accepted the offer, and amid a great deal of controversy a new Town Hall was built. Costing £7,300,
the building provided not merely a hall as originally intended, but council offices as well. The Town Hall is seen here in
1910 during the ceremonial proclamation of George V.

57. Hitchin's traditional markets in grains were still flourishing in the middle of the 19th century. In order to take advantage of the extra business the new railway line would bring, the newly-formed Market Company raised £2,000 for the building of a Corn Exchange. In 1853 the building was complete and the 30 stalls were all taken up by dealers. To supplement the running of the new venture the company leased the market tolls from the Crown for 31 years.

58.   The Hitchin Infirmary, later the North Herts. and South Beds. Hospital in Bedford Road, was established in 1840 under the energetic supervision of Dr. Frederick Hawkins. It was supported by endowments and voluntary subscriptions. Each subscriber of two guineas or more became a governor of the infirmary and was entitled to refer up to two in-patients and four out-patients for treatment every year. Despite the paternalistic nature of this system it marked a great improvement in the care of the seriously ill. The Infirmary is seen here at the turn of the century.

59.   In this view, *c.*1960, The Croft appears exactly as it did in a photograph taken 100 years earlier. The façade is 19th century but the building dates back a further 400 years, when it is thought to have been a woolstaplers' hall. The staplers were a select group of merchants with royal authority to trade in the market at Calais. The Croft was one of a number of old buildings in Bancroft sadly lost to the town in the 1960s. An illusion of its continued existence is created by the attempted reproduction of the old façade above the line of shop fronts.

60. A hundred and more years ago the buildings in Bancroft were private residences. Many, like The Croft, had spacious and attractive gardens behind them. If The Croft were indeed a woolstaplers' hall then there would have been much dealing in locally-produced fleeces in these grounds. In 1859 the house was bought by James Hack Tuke, a partner in the Hitchin Bank, now Barclays, and frequently consulted by the Government as a self-taught expert on the 'Irish Question'.

61. The Hermitage consisted of a rambling collection of buildings of different periods that grew up around a 16th-century barn. It possessed 40 rooms, including a priest hole. The gardens covered seven acres and were tended by three gardeners. The various parts of the divided estate were linked by tunnels under the roads. The developer who bought the buildings in 1927 was a double-bass player in the orchestra of the Rural Music Schools. For a short while before demolition he rented part of the building as offices to Mary Ibberson, the Schools' founder.

62. Frederic Seebohm (1833-1912). Frederic was born of a Quaker family in Yorkshire. He became an early commuter, living at Hitchin while studying Law in London. There have been Quakers in Hitchin since the middle of the 17th century and he was soon welcomed into their society. Whilst in Hitchin he was to marry Mary Ann, daughter of William Exton, a local banker. He is best remembered as a scholar and as a benefactor of the town. A blue plaque now commemorates him on a wall at the corner of Hermitage Road and Bancroft.

63. These gardens at The Hermitage in the time of Mr. Charles Prime were famous in the locality. Now they are gone, covered with bricks and concrete, a service area at the back of the shops on Hermitage Road. The road was cut in 1874 when Frederic Seebohm gave part of the Hermitage grounds to the town for the building of a more direct route to the station. Portmill Lane was narrow and Nightingale Road at that time was little more than a muddy track, unsuited to take the increasing volume of traffic.

64. The demolition of The Hermitage and the later shopping development has changed the character of this part of Hitchin almost beyond recognition. However, part of the fabric of the old Hermitage has survived, as seen here at the backs of shops in Bancroft on the Hermitage Road corner.

65. Originally part of the Hermitage estate, the Lodge with its overhanging roof supported on posts is something of a landmark in Hitchin. In 1912, a few years after this scene was photographed, the building was extended, and in 1948 the thatch replaced with cedar wood shingles. During the reroofing it was discovered that the original straw was still present under a more recent layer, and the whole was at least four feet thick.

66. Grove Mill was once one of five mills powered by the River Hiz during the 19th century. The mill was built in 1814 by John Ransom on the site of Shooting Mill, an earlier thatched building that had burned down. Grove Mill passed into the hands of John's son, Joshua, whose acrimonious disputes with the town's first Board of Health over sewage outfall into the river contributed to the Board's eventual collapse. In 1889 Grove Mill, like its predecessor caught fire. Partly destroyed, it was rebuilt and thereafter used as a factory. The mill stood near the railway embankment in what is now Grove Road.

67. This photograph shows William Ransom, the chemist, and members of his family at Fairfield, their home in Benslow Lane. The house later became the property of Esther Seebohm, daughter of Frederic Seebohm of The Hermitage. In 1952 she bequeathed it to the Rural Music Schools. The Schools were established in Hitchin by 1930 with the aim of helping people living in rural areas to learn how to play musical instruments and to sing. They now have a small hall attached, and give frequent concerts.

68. The Convalescent Home, Benslow, built for the German Hospital in Dalston, London. On 8 November 1907 the foundation stone was laid by Princess Louise Augusta of Schleswig Holstein. The *Hertfordshire Express* reported, 'The sun shone merrily and the conditions were wonderfully mild and pleasant'. The idyllic mood was not to last. Eight years later, after the outbreak of war, members of the Hitchin bench of magistrates petitioned the government to close the home which was, as they put it, in the 'entire control of alien enemies of the country'. The owners had apparently failed to douse their lights on the order of the local police. The building is now a private hospital.

69. A Carmelite Priory founded in 1317 flourished in Hitchin until the Reformation when, in the reign of Henry VIII, the monks were ordered to surrender the building to the Crown. Falling into disuse, the Priory was quarried for building material. What was left was purchased in 1548 by the Radcliffe family. Based on a design by Robert Adam the Priory was rebuilt in the 1770s, practically bankrupting the family in the process. Very little of the building shown on this 17th-century print survives.

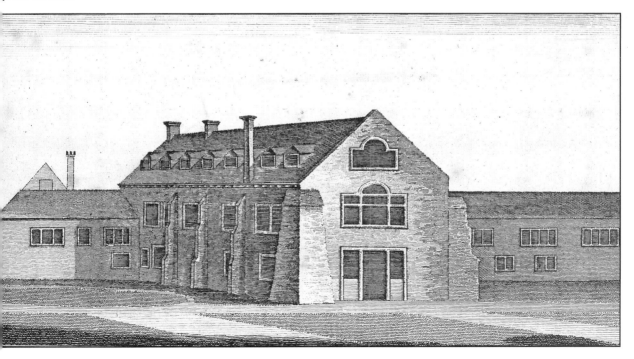

70. John Beaver, whose grocery shop was at 2 Market Place, was appointed Hitchin Postmaster in 1859 and continued as such for the next 40 years. Many changes occurred during his term of office: pillar boxes arrived, and in 1870 the electric telegraph was installed on the premises. He is here seen with his staff who are wearing the peaked caps which were part of a postman's uniform until 1898.

71. In 1900, on the death of John Beaver, Hitchin acquired its first full-time postmaster. Four years later, at a cost of £2,589, a new post office was completed in Brand Street next door to the Methodist chapel. The town's telephone exchange, previously housed in Tilehouse Street near the Priory entrance was transferred to the new building. The post office was to remain on this site for nearly 60 years, until it moved to Hermitage Road in 1962.

HITCHIN AREA.
HITCHIN.

9	ANSELL C. F.	Butcher,	91 Bancroft
4	CARLING W. & Co.	Printers & Publishers,	Exchange bldgs
14	COURTENAY J. W.	Wymondley House,	Stevanage
3	ELLIS & Evarard, Ld.	Merchants,	30 Bancroft
3a	ELLIS & Evarard, Ld.		Midland Goods yd
2	FLANDERS G. C.	Cycle Agent,	Tilehouse st
2a	FLANDERS G. C.	Cycle Agent,	Tilehouse st
11	HAWKINS & Co.	Solicitors,	
6	LOGSDON E.	Brewer, Jobmaster, Caterer,	Sun hotl
1	LOGSDON E.		Mkt pl
8	LUCAS W. & S., Ld.	Brewers,	Brewery
12	MOSS W. B.	Storekeeper,	High st
12a	MOSS W. B.	Storekeeper,	Nightingale rd
12b	MOSS W. B.	Warehouse & Stores,	Portmill rd
12c	MOSS W. B.	Warehouse & Stores,	Westbourne rd
12d	MOSS W. B.	Private Address :	Westbourne rd
13	NEWTON F.	Contractor, Plumber, &c.,	Tilehouse st
13a	NEWTON F.	Contractor, Plumber, &c.,	Tilehouse st
7	PHILLIPS F. W.	Dealer in Antiquities,	Manor ho
10	PIRKIS J. A.	Oil & Colorman,	Sun st
100	POST Office (for Postal Facilities **only**)		
5	SPENCER & Co.		Walsworth rd

72. The Hitchin telephone directory in 1901. Most of Hitchin's early telephone subscribers were local businesses, the name of W. B. Moss prominent among them. Moss, whose business acumen always served him well, was not slow to appreciate the value of the new invention. By 1911 the entries in the directory had risen to 70 and three telephonists had been employed to deal with the calls. But private subscribers were few in the early years; after all, there were not that many people to ring.

73. The Leeds to London Royal Mail coach passed through Hitchin for the first time in 1797. On the outward journey from London the coach rattled round the brewery corner in Sun Street a few minutes before midnight. It was allowed five minutes to change horses at the *Sun Inn* before continuing its journey. The horses were changed every 10 miles. By Queen Victoria's reign the coach was achieving average speeds of 10 miles per hour, the entire journey taking 21 hours in all.

74. Hitchin Fire Brigade collected its first steam-powered pump from Hitchin railway station on 21 April 1887. The captain at the time was Isaac Chalkley, who stands at the lower right of the picture. They then drove their new engine to the *Sun Hotel* followed by their colleagues from Baldock, stopped to pose for Mr. Latchmore's camera, and then continued to the Priory Park, where they gave the town a demonstration of the steamer's water-raising capacity.

75.   In 1895 Isaac Chalkley retired and was succeeded by Edwin Logsdon as captain of the brigade. The new chief, a forthright and energetic man, was largely responsible for raising the £711 required to build the new fire station in Paynes Park. The council, which had recently leased the land from Trinity College, Cambridge for the new cattle market, gave the plot, together with a donation of £211. Trinity College gave a further £50. Logsdon stands nearest the camera on one of the brigade's manual engines, outside the new station. Behind the engine is a single horse carriage which carries hose wound on a drum beneath the seat.

76. Captain Loftus Barham's dedication to the brigade was such that until he was admitted to a London hospital on 29 July 1921, shortly before his death, he had not spent a single night away from home for 34 years in case a fire should call him from his bed. Two days later his coffin was brought back to Hitchin on the brigade's Mercedes, the tractor unit for their steam pump. His family gave consent for the brigade to organise the funeral in order that his wish to die a fireman might be fulfilled.

77. On 24 June 1850 an announcement appeared in Hitchin to the effect that in future shops would be closed at the earlier time of 8.00 p.m. Despite this improvement, the long hours worked by shop assistants was a matter for public concern, and led to the founding of the Hitchin Early Closing Association. Members are seen here on the Association's float for Queen Victoria's Diamond Jubilee celebrations. The aim was to achieve a voluntary reduction of hours by shopkeepers, and members worked at persuading ordinary citizens not to leave their shopping until late in the evening.

78. In 1906 the Hitchin Parliamentary Division sent a Liberal politician to Westminster. Four
years later the election of the Conservative candidate, Dr. Alfred Hillier, was greeted with scenes
of tumultuous rejoicing among his supporters. On leaving the old Town Hall after the
announcement, the horses of Dr. Hillier's carriage were unhitched and he was pulled all around
the town and back to the Conservative Club in Sun Street. That night a hastily-arranged
torchlight procession was held in the streets. The events reached a tragic conclusion, when the
following year Dr. Hillier committed suicide.

79.   In September 1915 and again in January 1916 Zeppelins were seen over the town, and bombs were dropped in Walsworth and Bedford Roads. Captain Barham, who saw the fire brigade through the war years, amassed the collection of bombs seen in this photograph.

80.   The Walsworth Platoon of the Home Guard in the rain. Every Sunday during the Second World War members assembled on a small shooting range behind the Priory for bomb throwing and target practice – as well as a chat and an exchange of news.

81.   On 10 August 1850 the first Great Northern Railway train ran from London and Peterborough through Hitchin. The two platforms of the early station were connected by a narrow and often windy passenger bridge, which came to be known as 'The Hitchin Alps'. This photograph, taken in about 1866, shows the station looking south. Engine no. 53, built by Hawthorn of Newcastle, is standing at the up platform.

82.   An early suggestion for the site of the new railway station was the top of Brand Street where the Town Hall now stands. A story is told that the Quakers, whose Meeting House was close by, objected to the plan: however, the reason why the station was eventually built a mile outside the town remains uncertain. The public were informed that 'Omnibuses and flys are announced to meet every train', and flys and cabs may be had from the *Sun Hotel* and the *Cock Hotel'*.

83. Staff and cabs outside the new station. In the early 20th century the number of passengers at Hitchin had increased dramatically; employees of firms on the new Letchworth industrial estate and City commuters swelled the daily traffic. By 1911 the station's facilities were clearly inadequate and Hitchin Urban District Council persuaded the reluctant Great Northern Railway Company to make major alterations. As a result the station buildings were completely remodelled on the western side. The huge canopy survived until 1980 when, full of dry rot and a danger to passengers, it was demolished.

84. The down platform of Hitchin station after 1911. The most obvious change that has taken place is the removal of the bridge, and the construction of a new wide passenger underpass, but platforms have also been lengthened and deepened. In the distance is Benslow Bridge which was demolished on 28 July 1974 at 1.37 a.m., during electrification of the line.

85. The *Angel Vaults Inn* and its neighbour the *Sun*, in 1870. Though the date 1450 appeared on the façade of the *Angel*, the roof construction appeared to be considerably older. In the mid 1950s a beam and some plaster fell in the main part of the building and disturbing noises were heard up in the lofts. Three consecutive roofs had been built, one on top of another in the old building, and its main 14th-century beam was broken. The inn was declared unsafe and was demolished at once.

86. The Elizabethan yard of the *Sun Hotel*. The *Sun* was at one time almost self supporting: it had its own farm which provided fresh meat, fruit and vegetables for its busy kitchens. It grew its own hops and brewed its own beer. Once it even boasted a medicinal spring which was said to 'purge very kindly ... and was of great effect in cholicks'. It is said that the inn played host to both Oliver Cromwell and King Henry VIII, and during the Napoleonic wars the Hitchin Loyal Volunteers guarded 250 French prisoners in the yard.

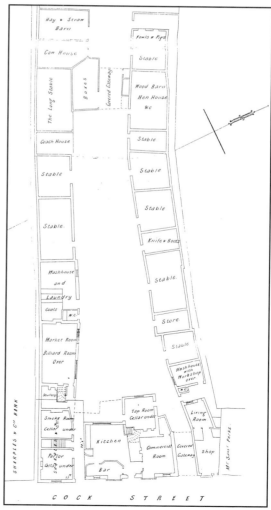

87 & 88. By the end of the 18th century the *Cock*, kept by Jane Allbury, was the town's principal inn. Coaches clattered regularly in and out of its busy yard. Built in 1563, possibly on stone foundations quarried from the old Priory, the inn derived its name from the cockfighting which was once offered as a regular entertainment. A 19th-century bill of sale describes the *Cock* as having three parlours, a dairy, a mangling room, 10 bedchambers, and a soldiers' room. At the rear two large yards provided stabling for 68 horses, with lofts and granaries over, two barns, a double coach house, piggeries, wood and coal houses, a garden and a dung pit. Two-thirds of the building was pulled down in the early 1930s to make way for a new store. The plan shows the extent of the inn and its yards in the 19th century.

89 & 90. The *Swan Hotel* in Market Place dates from 1539 and was a popular eating place on market days. Jonas Kershaw, proprietor of the Hitchin stagecoach, which set out for London several times a week, was landlord until 1805. The coaching arch bears the name of a later publican, William Lewin, and advertises 'Horses and Carriages for hire'. In the yard beyond, now the site of The Arcade, many tradesmen plied their craft. In 1878 William Beaver, brother of the postmaster, made baskets, Alfred Rogers had a coach-building workshop and there were coopers, saddlers, ostlers and harness-makers. The *Swan* was a place of popular entertainment; 2d. melodramas drew large crowds, and in August 1865 the inn presented 'the extraordinary blue and flesh coloured hairless horse from the South of Africa'. Gatwards the ironmongers, who occupied the premises next door and already had an iron foundry in the *Swan* yard, bought the old inn in 1884 for £3,715. Outside the entrance is a member of the 2nd (Hitchin) Division of the Hertfordshire police force. Further down the road Barclays has not yet extended its Italianate façade.

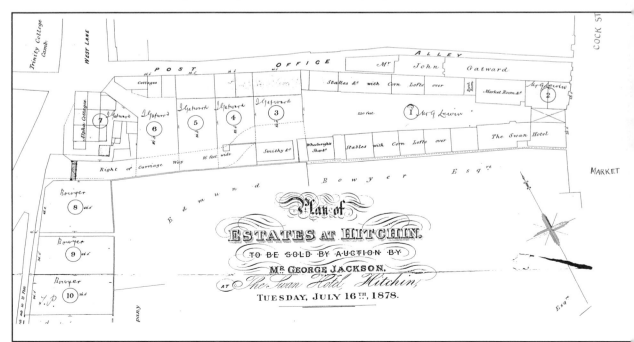

91.   The building that is now the *George* in Bucklersbury is one of the oldest in Hitchin, dating back to about 1450. It was probably built as the home of a rich merchant, but became an inn at least by 1676 under the name of the *Falcon*. In 1870 as the *Beehive* it lost its licence, and the building was taken over by the *George*, formerly located in the High Street. On market days straw plaiters and plait dealers gathered here to do business along with the farmers. The balustrade in this photograph is all that survives of a long gallery.

92.   Tilehouse or 'Tylers' Street, in which the *Coopers Arms* stands, was once probably occupied by brickmakers, and it is possible that the pub was once a tylers' guildhall. Fine mullioned windows at the rear of the building date it to the 15th century. In an early map the building is shown standing detached on an open green. Stories about the *Coopers Arms* abound. It is said that there is a tunnel, now bricked up, that once connected the building with the Priory, and its strange noises and spectral monks are all part of the town's mythology. The building was once owned by William Lucas, the brewer, but there is no record of a pub licence before 1860.

93.   Two old inns standing side by side in Bancroft were frequented by drovers and farmers during the many years the livestock market was held in the street outside. The *Crown* was built in 1654; the *White Lion* was probably from the same period. For a while the *Crown* was a parcels depot for the Great Northern Railway. When both inns were demolished in 1966 they continued for a few years as the *Crown and Lion* before giving way to a supermarket.

94 & 95. Several pubs opened close to the station hoping to take advantage of the trade that the railways would bring. The *Railway Inn* was built by W. & S. Lucas, the Sun Street brewers. In later years the stables were pulled down and the building enlarged. In 1965 the inn became known as the *Talisman*, after a train that ran non-stop between London and Edinburgh. The sober outline of the *Railway Inn* is not immediately recognisable in its last incarnation as *Jeans*, which survived for a few short, energetic years before being closed in the mid-1980s. The building was demolished in 1991.

96. The *Woolpack* at Starling's Bridge celebrating the coronation of Edward VII, in 1902. The pub was built *c.*1840 by W. Foss, a wool sorter by trade, on what was then the very edge of the town. The last working forge in Hitchin was in the *Woolpack* yard.

97. The *Falcon*, *c*.1890. This house in Park Street stood alone when it was built in 1660. Being outside the town it was used at one time as a pest house or isolation hospital. In 1857 it was bought by Fordhams, the Ashwell brewers. Mr. Fordham established a forge there in 1860 and worked as a publican and blacksmith. His son, James Ellis Fordham, continued the business, beginning work every morning at 5 a.m. shoeing horses. It was said that he could tell who had shod a horse by its hoof marks. The building later became a garage and was demolished in July 1950.

98. The *Ship* at Walsworth has been serving beer since at least 1806. It has been rebuilt twice since that time, once in 1901 and then again in 1950. In this photograph taken in 1926 a game of bowls is in progress on the three-rink green built by Jacob Gillett, a former publican. Sports were evidently a feature at the *Ship*; an advertisement for the pub in 1899 offers: 'Good accommodation for Cyclists or Beanfeasts. Terms Moderate. Good Quoit ground'.

99.   In 1851 the *Cricketers* was the only building on Bedford Road between the Butts Close corner and the track that is now Bearton Road. At that time it occupied the building shown in this photograph which is now the *Firs Hotel*. While on this earlier site the *Cricketers* doubled as a changing room for the football club when it played on the Top Field opposite. The photograph, taken in 1905, shows Pryor Reid, the Hatfield brewers, delivering to the *Cricketers* in a small steam wagon. On the back of the wagon are bags of coal for the engine's boiler.

100. The Reverend George Gainsford (1829-1910) came to Hitchin in 1852 as a young man, to take up his first curacy at the parish church of St Mary's. He remained for two years, long enough to marry Annette Wiley, the vicar's daughter. Ten years later, he returned to build a new church in Radcliffe Road. In 1864, amid fields of corn, the foundation stone of St Saviour's was laid by his wife. He was much respected: at his death huge crowds gathered by the graveside, and all trading in the town ceased for the day.

101. In 1910 George Gainsford's son, George Bernard (1868-1933), followed his father as vicar of St Saviour's. George Bernard's energy was enormous. Beside his ecclesiastical duties he served as chairman of the Urban District Council from 1925 to 1928; he was a founder member of Hitchin Light Opera Company, later the Thespians, and from time to time he played football for Hitchin Town. His interest in mechanical things led him to become one of Hitchin's first motorists and a member of North Herts. Motoring Club.

102. For the design of St Saviour's, George Gainsford obtained the services of William Butterfield, a favoured architect of the Oxford Movement. The church was built in a rapidly-expanding area of the town to meet the needs of the new residents. It was an immediate success: congregations became so large that two aisles were added in the 1880s to accommodate them, and in 1865 Queen Victoria signed the deed that constituted St Saviour's as a separate parish. The building was to become, for a number of years, the 'society' church in preference to St Mary's, which was then surrounded by slum dwellings.

103.   While studying at Oxford in the early 1850s George Gainsford was influenced by John Henry Newman and the Tractarian Movement. The Movement attempted to breathe new life into the Established Church by bringing it closer to the Church of Rome. Harvest festivals, then unknown in the Church of England, elaborate vestments and processions with banners and icons of the Virgin caused quite a stir in Hitchin and stimulated a heated correspondence in the local paper. In this photograph, taken in 1909, George Gainsford is seen with his son and the choir at the back of St Saviour's church.

104.   By 1869 the efforts of George Gainsford and his churchwardens had raised the sum of £295 13s. 3d. for the building of a school for both boys and girls. The school was erected in the fields opposite the church. Gainsford himself contributed £20. A few years later, in 1873, an orphanage was built next door 'for poor girls whose fathers are dead or have deserted them and cannot be found'. In this photograph of the school taken in 1929, the children from the orphanage are easily identified by the uniform that they wear.

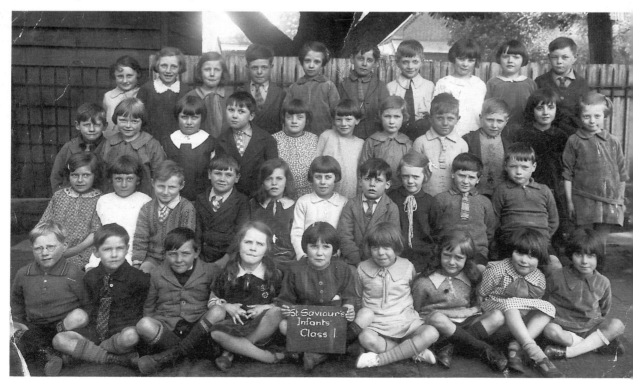

105. In 1867 Richard Johnson, a Baptist and chief engineer of the Great Northern Railway, erected a hall in Walsworth
Road as a centre for his mission work in this newly-built area of the town near the station. The unprepossessing iron hall,
seen here in 1869, was the butt of some ridicule but the congregation increased sufficiently in two years to form a new
church. The road in this photograph was in due course to become Highbury Hill, while Benslow Lane is seen disappearing
through the gateway on the left.

106. In July 1875 the work of Johnson and his colleagues led to the building of a new and much more substantial Baptist church next to the mission hall. This new church was designed to seat a congregation of 730, indicating the extent of Johnson's success. Many members of this early congregation were railway workers.

107. In 1904 the Caldicott School was established behind the Walsworth Road Baptist church as a preparatory school for the Leys in Cambridge. The 1909 guide to the town says that the school 'though distinctly nonconformist in tone arranges for boys of Church of England parents to attend their own place of worship'. The school moved to Farnham in 1938, and the building is now used as a youth club funded by the Hitchin Youth Trust (formerly the Hitchin Youth Association Ltd.), with money raised by the sale of nearby land.

108. The Salvation Army arrived in Hitchin in 1888 characteristically determined not to be put off by hostility directed at them from certain sections of the community. The foundation stone of their new Barracks was laid in Taylors Lane (now Florence Street). 'Some hustling by roughs' was reported. The Army became a familiar sight in the Market Place on Sundays. The building is now a warehouse used by Waters, the removals firm.

109. An enthusiastic welcome for General William Booth, founder of the Salvation Army, in Brand Street in July 1908, during one of his long tours of the country which, on this occasion, had begun in Dundee. While in the town he spoke in the Town Hall of the evils of alcohol and the work of the Salvation Army. Supporters of Hitchin's strong temperance movement gave him a standing ovation.

> ### To the Catholics of HITCHIN and Neighbourhood.
>
> ---
>
> There is Holy Mass at 10-30, on Sunday next and every Sunday, except for the present on the first Sunday of the Month, at Mr. Hutchinson's, Nightingale Road, Hitchin.
>
> All Catholics are exhorted to use the opportunity thus given of hearing Holy Mass and approaching the Sacraments.
>
> *Tuesday.* November 25th, 1890.
>
> *Sunday Nov. 30th 1890*
> *First Mass ? 1st Sunday of Advent.*
> *St Andrews day*

110. In 1870, one of a group of Catholic missionary priests from Barnet began work in Hitchin and the surrounding area. By 1890 there was sufficient interest to begin holding Sunday Mass at a house in Nightingale Road. Later the Mass Centre moved to 64 Old Park Road. This upstairs room was hardly sufficient for the needs of the small congregation; it was so tiny that some members had to kneel on the stairs during the service. A visit by Cardinal Vaughan to these cramped quarters in 1897 led quickly to a decision to build a church.

111. In 1899 the Catholic community purchased a plot of land for £320 on the corner of Grove and Nightingale Roads, mid-way between the old and new parts of the town. Three years later a church was erected. In about 1902 French Edmundian fathers pressured out of their native country by anti-clerical laws, made their way to England and took up their duties at the new church of Mary Immaculate and St Andrew in Hitchin. The church is shown in this view before the bell tower was built in about 1907.

112. In 1903 the Edmundian fathers transferred their school, founded on Mont Saint Michel in northern Brittany, to a building near the church in Hitchin. Though the staff were French, they appointed an English headmaster and tried to make the school as English as possible. Meeting other schools and local firms on the playing fields helped to break down barriers between the new Catholic community and the town. By 1906 the school, St Michael's College, had moved into a new building nearby, seen here shortly after its completion. The school moved to Stevenage in 1968 and the building was demolished three years later. A police station now occupies the site.

113. In 1690, with new freedoms of worship granted under the Act of Toleration, a group of Independents in the Hitchin area purchased an orchard in Dead Street from Widow Bonfield, and built a meeting house there. In 1856, despite financial difficulties, a new chapel was erected in the Italianate style on land fronting the road, and the old building was converted into a schoolroom. This old building, seen here, was demolished in 1869.

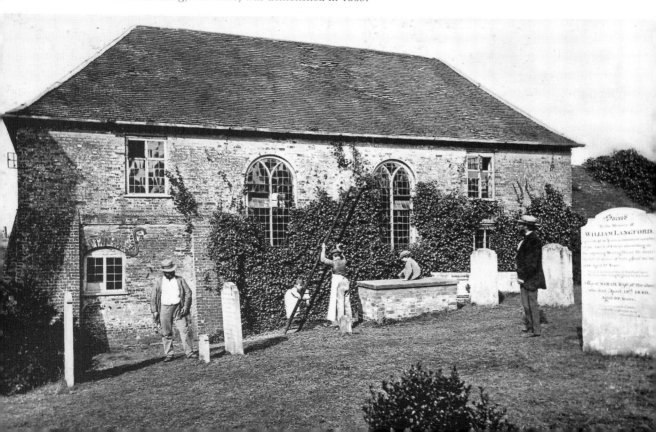

114. Girls at drill in the playground of the British School in Queen Street. Though they were non-denominational, the British School tended to flourish in towns such as Hitchin where non-conformity was well-established and influential. The building facing Queen Street today dates from 1857 but the school goes back to 1810 when William Wilshere, a Hitchin lawyer, founded an educational establishment for boys in a disused tannery. Nine years later a girls' school was added. A fee of 1d. per week was charged for attending and a strict code of dress was enforced. A notable feature of the building is the gallery classroom, which is thought to be the sole survivor of its kind in the country.

115.   In opposition to the view that women have 'mobile nervous systems which would break down under serious mental culture' the country's first all-female college of a university standard was founded at Benslow House, Hitchin in 1869. Hitchin was chosen for its convenient railway links with Cambridge and London, enabling lecturers to visit from the two universities. Four years later the school moved to Cambridge where it became Girton College. This photograph shows students outside Benslow House in 1872.

116. During the 19th century Perks' chemist shop in the High Street established a world-wide reputation for its lavender products, including Prize Medal Lavender Water, scented soaps, shampoos, and smelling salts. In 1871 the shop bought up Merrick's, the drapers next door. Rising labour costs were responsible for the decline of the business in the middle of the 20th century and in 1961 the last proprietor, Miss V. Lewis, sold the High Street premises to Woolworth's.

117. During the harvest, cropped lavender was brought from the fields into Perks' cobbled yard behind the shop. There women and children sat removing the stalks so that only the blooms would be consigned to the stills. Once in the still the blooms would be trodden down to pack in as much as possible. Observers have remarked that during this process the aroma of the lavender became so strong as to be almost unendurable.

118. Miss Lewis made a collection of artefacts connected with the lavender industry. When her business in High Street was sold the contents of the shop were removed and established as a museum in Lucas Lane. Since May 1990 the reconstructed Victorian chemist shop with its original fittings has been on display in Hitchin Museum.

119. An early interest in chemistry grafted onto a family farming tradition led William Ransom (1826-1914) to found his pharmaceutical business in Bancroft and Sun Street. The firm was unusual in that it grew as well as distilled many of its herbal extracts. Like a number of other Quaker businessmen in the town, Ransom's interests ranged widely. Besides being a pharmaceutical chemist he was an antiquarian of some note, and was responsible for excavations of a Roman villa near Hitchin.

120. Ransom's lavender fields during the August harvest, c.1900. The plant was cropped just as the flowers began to fade, for that was the time when the oil content was at its greatest. From that moment all available workers on the farm and in the factory turned out into the fields. Within a week the entire crop had been cut, distilled and bottled. One ton of lavender yielded 20 lb. of oil which was later diluted to produce lavender water. Ransom's 20 acres annually produced 1,000 gallons of the final product.

121. In the early days of the business, over 150 different herbs were cultivated on the Ransom's farm just outside Hitchin. In this photograph, taken around the turn of the century, workers are harvesting a crop of deadly nightshade. Whole families often worked in the fields together year after year. The Ransom farm has now been sold to Stevenage Development Corporation, but herbs are still grown today at the firm's fields near St Ives, Cambridgeshire.

122. Some of Ransom's Victorian distilling apparatus is still in use today, side by side with modern technology. Once in the factory the herbs are ground, placed in digesters, covered with alcohol or water and left to soften. The liquid extracts are then drawn off and evaporated. Here soft extracts of plants such as liquorice and Quassia stems are taken to completion in steam-heated evaporating pans.

123. Ransom's bottling plant c.1946, before the introduction of modern machinery. In the background are barrels of liquid extracts. Two of the labels show the contents to be cascara, a South American bark, and belladonna, otherwise known as deadly nightshade. Until 1975 the products were kept in stock vessels such as these and bottled up as ordered.

124. The tannery works of G. W. Russell and Son occupied a site in Bancroft from the early 19th century, though the origins of the firm can be traced back to at least 1775. Before the Second World War, Russell's, specialising in sheep skins, used methods familiar to tanners since the earliest times. After chemical treatment loosened wool was 'pulled' from the pelts before being sent to Bradford for spinning. Next the pelts were soaked in limepits for about a fortnight. In this photograph, taken in the 1920s, shammys are being beaten by heavy hammers known as 'stocks', covered with cod oil, then beaten again until they are thoroughly impregnated.

125. In the leather-making process the whole thickness of the skin is not always used. Often it is split horizontally into layers of which only the top one bears the natural grain. This layer known as the 'skiver' is used for belts, the insides of shoes, and so forth. The lower or flesh split produces shammys which once went to make large numbers of ladies' white gloves. By a different process fine splits were turned into parchment, much of which was sent to America for students' degree certificates. In this photograph shammys are being graded and then finished over an emery wheel to buff them up on both sides.

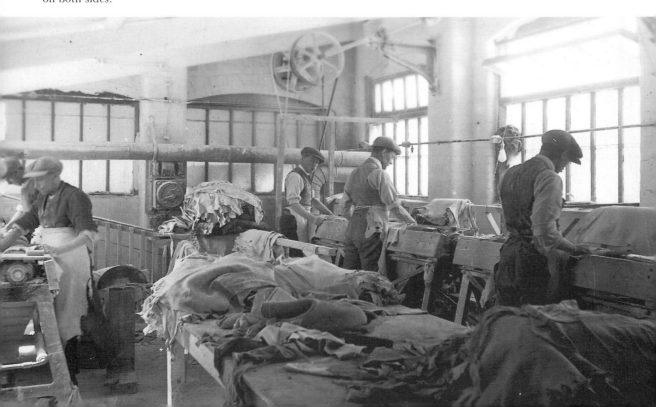

126. Before the Second World War Russell's owned a field near Pirton Road. Here a gang of workers has arrived with a lorry-load of shammy leathers which they are laying out to bleach in the sun. The skins used before the Second World War were usually English, being preferred for quality over those from Australia or New Zealand. After the War there were a number of changes in the methods used. Shammys were no longer laid out in this way but bleached in sulphur stoves at the tannery.

127. Whereas shammys were tanned with fish oil, 'skivers' were usually saturated with an infusion of Sicilian sumach leaves. On the left of this photograph leathers are being 'sleaked' with a flat steel blade. This stretches them and removes any remaining traces of the tanning solution. In the firm's early days this process was always done by hand. On the right are drums that were used for dying the leathers.

128.   A young apprentice wheelman at Russells during the 1920s. Buffing the shammys was a skilled job and apprenticeships to the trade lasted five years. At that time an apprentice's pay was as low as 2d. per hour. Russells was bought out in 1952 by another tanning firm based in Bermondsey. When it in turn was taken over in 1986/7 the Hitchin factory was closed.

129.   The firm of Harkness and Sons, nurserymen, came from North Yorkshire to set up a branch at Charlton in 1892, where it specialised in growing roses. After a spell at Oakfield Farm, on what is now the Oakfield Housing Estate, it moved to its present site on Letchworth Road, known locally as Rose Hill. Robert Harkness, one of the sons, ran the Oakfield and Letchworth Road farms with great success, establishing the firm of R. Harkness and Co. in 1901. These ornamental display gardens of the late 1960s were a local landmark until economic circumstances made it necessary for the land to revert to general agricultural use, though nearby fields still provide a riot of colour every year.

130. Keeping down weeds is one of the major tasks of rose nurseries, for the plants remain undisturbed through two growing seasons. In this photograph of 1928, Ernest Worbey is steering his hoe between the rows. The horse wears protective material made out of cyclists' leggings on its forelegs to guard against rose thorns, while the string muzzle protects the roses from the horse.

131. Ena Harkness (1906-90): the face behind a famous rose. Ena's name became a household word after the introduction of a red rose named for her in 1946. The rose was raised by Albert Norman, a friend of the Harkness family. She was a director of the firm for over 30 years and won an international reputation as a flower arranger, lecturer and judge.

132. During the Second World War Harkness were required to turn over all but one acre of their land to the growing of food crops. In this advertisement the familiar rose has given way to the humble, but life-sustaining, potato.

133. The brewery, founded in 1709 by the Quaker brothers William and Joseph Lucas and brother-in-law Isaac Grey, dominated the corner of Sun Street and Bridge Street for over 200 years: it was the most important in a town noteworthy for its brewers and maltsters. William Lucas, the diarist, struggled hard with his conscience over the nature of the family business in the mid-19th century, but the sons continued to go into the firm and expanded its operations to New York and Chicago. The Hitchin site was busy with coopers, bottlers, brewers and carpenters working in a cluster of buildings overlooking the Hiz.

134. Lucas drays and lorries were a familiar sight delivering beer, spirits and bottled, aerated water around the town. At least 10 Hitchin pubs were supplied by the firm. Employees of W. and S. Lucas are here seen standing beside the firm's Foden steam wagon in 1910. Thirteen years later, changes in the economic climate and the results of water shortages in the drought years of the early 1920s were to kill off the business. The old buildings finally came down in 1963 making way for Crown House, the Hitchin offices of the Inland Revenue.

135. John Cannon's Chalkdell nurseries near the Hitchin Hospital was one of a number of similar businesses that flourished throughout the 19th and early 20th centuries. This photograph was taken in the mid-1930s. Fifty years earlier, Grove Road and Bancroft Recreation Ground were the site of an extensive business owned by John Fells. Other nurseries appear on the 1881 Ordnance Survey map at the top of Dacre and Trevor Roads. The growing of geraniums was a Hitchin speciality.

136 & 137. The making of straw plait for the Luton and Dunstable hatteries was an important industry in Hitchin until the end of the 19th century. In these two photographs women demonstrate the method of plaiting split straws or 'splints'. Plaiting was a considerably healthier occupation than many other cottage industries in that it could be pursued in the open air and did not tax the eyesight, as did lacemaking, for example. The women often gathered in the streets to talk while working almost mechanically with their fingers, producing endless ribbons of plait. As can be seen from these photographs, they took considerable pride in their dress, which won for them an undeserved reputation among the middle classes for loose morals.

38. As much as £1,000-worth of plait changed hands in one day's trading at Hitchin market, held traditionally in the outh-west corner of the Market Place before the demise of the industry at the end of the 19th century. The completed plait an be seen stuffed into bags at the front of the picture. Hitchin market attracted plaiters from many of the outlying villages nd dealers from as far away as Essex, where there was also a small plait-making industry. Hitchin market paid higher rices for the finished product, as it was nearer to the hat-making towns.

139. In this photograph of the Bancroft osier beds taken in 1877, James Bullard stands on the left with a bunch of peeled withies ready to take back to his shop in Churchyard. In 1906 his son, who continued the business, advertised baskets, 'art' furniture, bottle cases, and 'plain and fancy' wicker-work. William Beaver, whose premises were in the *Swan* yard, stands on the other side of the path. On the right a group of youths are peeling the cut osiers, a tedious task, while in the foreground Mr. Abbis is bundling them in a clamp. Bancroft recreation ground, laid out in 1929 at a cost of £8,000, now occupies the site.

140. Francis Newton's of Tilehouse Street is the oldest building company in Hitchin, possibly in the country. Founded in the early 18th century the firm has occupied the same premises for over 250 years. The family was descended from the younger brother of Sir Isaac Newton, the philosopher and scientist.

141. Newton's workshops were in an extensive yard opposite their Tilehouse Street offices. Before the Second War the quality of work that a building firm achieved depended almost entirely on its own employees: everything, even paint, had to be made up from its basic ingredients. Each of these men in Newton's joinery shop was a highly skilled craftsman in his own right. The workshops survived until the mid-1950s when a huge blaze destroyed almost everything in the yard, including a medieval tithe barn.

142. Newton's engraved business card. The joint calling of 'painter, plumber and glazier' was a common one from at least the 16th century until the middle of the 19th. The link between these various occupations is a skill in the safe handling of that hazardous substance, lead: lead as a base for paint, lead for the making of water pipes, and lead for making both glass and the 'cames' into which it is fixed.

143. Pumps, water pipes and coffin linings all were made from lead, as were church roofs. Newton's was responsible for leading St Mary's at least as far back as 1775 and the firm's daybooks show that every church within a 10-mile radius of Hitchin was re-roofed by them at some time. Milled lead was available from London and sometimes used, but it was expensive and its great weight made it difficult to transport – especially in the days before the steam engine. Whenever possible old lead was recast in the firm's own furnace, shown here in their Tilehouse Street workshops, before 1896.

144. Newton's sign can be seen on the lashed wood scaffolding during repairs to the Priory. Until recent times Hitchin was almost self-sufficient in building materials. The timber scaffolding would quite probably have come from the woods at Redcoats Green. Sand came from what is now the open-air theatre near Windmill Hill; lime from the dells on the land sloping up to Benslow; and bricks were made on a site where the Sunnyside estate now stands.

145. At the turn of the century the firm of P. H. Barker, specialists in high-class joinery, had already been established at the top of Hermitage Road. By 1966 the mills were transferred to Cadwell Lane near the Midland Railway embankment, where they were to become the nucleus of a new industrial estate. The Norman vessel standing behind the group of workers was being built for the Conservative Working Men's Association as their contribution to King George V's coronation celebrations.

146. In 1849 Walter Odell, son of Robert Odell, the Bridge Street farrier, set up as a coachbuilder in Portmill Lane. Later he returned to Bridge Street to open the 'Carriage Repository' with his brother. In 1898 the Repository was sold to Ralph E. Sanders, while Walter, a studious man, went on to establish a second-hand bookshop and lending library in the churchyard. Nevertheless, he remained an expert valuer and adviser on the subject of carriages and wrote regularly for 'Exchange and Mart'.

147. Ralph Sanders, who had already opened a coachbuilding works in Royston, developed Odell's business at the 'Repository', manufacturing carriages, cycles and motor cars. Later the firm was to diversify into wirelesses as well, with premises in the High Street. In this photograph of the coachworks a splendid selection of broughams and landaus is being offered for sale. A dogcart stands in the centre of the photograph.

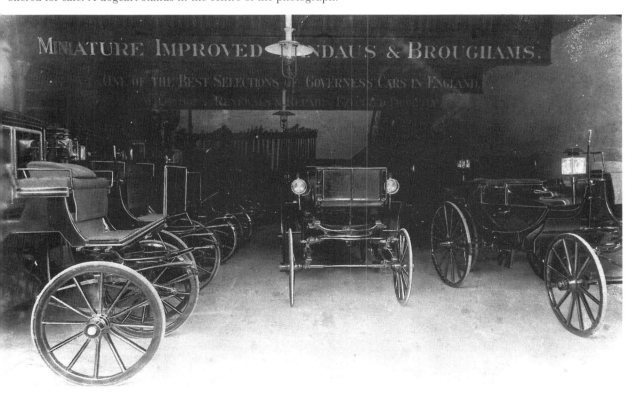

Tele. 91.

RALPH E. SANDERS & SONS Lᵀᴰ

Motor Agents & Engineers

HITCHIN, HERTS.

The "FORD" DELIVERY VAN

148. The advent of the motor car posed new problems for the coachbuilder. At first they were able to adapt their traditional craft to the new vehicles by providing car bodies for the engineering firms who manufactured the engine and chassis. In their 1910 brochure Sanders offers to provide 'special designs embodying enquirer's suggestions', warning that after each outing 'the Car should be thoroughly washed down the moment it gets home, otherwise the varnish will be spotted with mud stains'. Here the firm is advertising on the side of a vehicle which consists of a van body attached to a Ford chassis.

149. Sanders was able successfully to adapt to the motor car. In 1906 it opened a new garage in Walsworth Road, close to the station, and the following year they were to build new premises in Royston. With the arrival of mass production they gave up coachbuilding altogether and became a retail outlet for motor vehicles. The Walsworth Road garage, seen here within a few years of its completion, was one of the first of its kind in the country.

150.   In 1859 John Moss, a travelling draper, rented a shop in Bancroft where the magistrates' court now stands. The shop which was managed by his wife, took a meagre 30s. in its first week's trading. In 1868 W. B. Moss took over the business from his father, and by 1927 the firm had 12 branches in the area and a large warehouse in Portmill Lane where they bagged tea and flour, killed their own pigs, and made pork pies and sausages.

151.   Towards the end of the 19th century Moss's bought a 17th-century house at the head of Bancroft that had formerly been the *Trooper Inn*. Their business sense became legendary. The marriage notice of W. H. Moss (W. B.'s son) to Fanny Tetley was concluded in the local newspaper with the following: 'W. B. Moss's Meat Dept. – Pork is now in season; fresh joints and sausages daily'. In 1899 Moss's demolished the *Trooper* to make way for a larger building – the one we have today. During the work a large number of human skeletons were found, suggesting the site was formerly a graveyard, probably belonging to a religious order.

152. Tom Brooker, originally from a farming family, came to Hitchin in 1876 and set up an ironmongery business on the corner of Walsworth and Dacre Roads. He paid £176 15s. 6d. for the building, with the intention of having another storey added later. The two boys in the picture are Arthur and Tom Brooker, who were to expand the business into one of Hitchin's largest concerns. This photograph was taken for inclusion in the 1911 coronation souvenir brochure. The photographer has whited out or otherwise marked areas he wishes to eliminate, including a sign advertising a neighbouring business.

153. Before concentrating their business in the Bucklersbury premises, Brooker's also had a shop in Sun Street. The firm sold a wide variety of items, large and small, such as lawnmowers, mangles, baths, gas and bell fittings and kitchen ranges as well as offering to repair furniture or remake bedding. Terry Brooker stands in the centre of this group.

154. George Hawkins opened his clothier and outfitter's shop at 6 Bucklersbury in 1863. The business has grown over the years and now occupies several of the adjoining premises. In the window are rows of watches and loose collars, as well as various garments for sale.

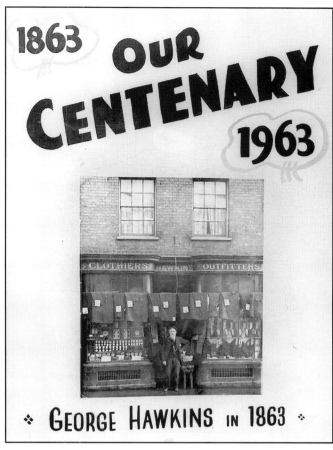

155. Nicholls', milliners and drapers, a familiar sight in Bancroft until recent times, acquired this building in 1920 and put in plate-glass windows – some of the first to appear in Bancroft. The addition was welcomed by the *Hertfordshire Express* as a 'brightening up' of the street, as no doubt it was after the rigours of the First World War. During the War the building had been used as a quartermaster's stores for the army stationed at Bearton Camp.

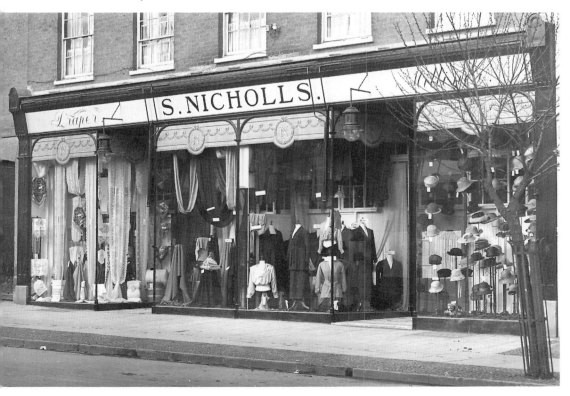

156. Religious, trade union, and political banners were very much in demand at a time when life was more public than it is today. Herbert Sharp, banner-maker, came to Hitchin in 1940 when the premises of his employer in London were bombed. In 1946 he opened a studio in Tilehouse Street and set up his own business. The banners in this photograph, depicting 'King Billy', are no doubt destined for an orange lodge in Northern Ireland.

157. A modern view of the High Street, with the familiar Italianate façade of Barclays Bank. When Pierson's Bank, a private local business, failed in 1841, the site was purchased by Sharples, Exton and Lucas and a new building was erected. Joseph Sharples and William Exton were Quaker businessmen, directors of a bank based in Leighton Buzzard, which had begun as a sideline to a grocer's shop. They moved to Hitchin in 1827 to run their Hitchin Branch as a separate business.

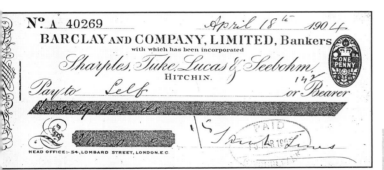

158. Having married two sisters, Sharples and Exton both came into property in Bancroft. Members of other Quaker families joined the business: Jeffrey, Edward and Francis Lucas of the brewing family in Sun Street, James Hack Tuke, owner of The Croft, and Frederic Seebohm all became partners at various times. Eventually a number of private banks, mostly of Quaker origin, formed themselves into a Joint Stock Company under the name of Barclay and Co. Ltd. This was truly a family affair as both Joseph Gurney Barclay and Frederic Seebohm were married to William Exton's daughters.

159. The Blue Cross Brigade began in 1874 as a temperance organisation, running bible, book-keeping and shorthand classes. Its aims were to 'promote the physical, mental, moral and spiritual welfare of the members'. The Brigade became a well-known social club with its own club house and gymnasium at the top of Brand Street. Its gymnastic team was in popular demand for all sorts of events.

160.   Hitchin's first baths in Queen Street cost £742 4s. 4d. to build in 1860. They were filled directly from the nearby Hiz and their murky contents discharged once a week back into the river. The baths were popular from the beginning. They opened from April to November from 5.30 in the morning till 9.00 at night, suggesting the hours kept by the inhabitants of a 19th-century country town. Admission was 3d. and three mornings a week were reserved for ladies only. Following the opening of the new swimming pool in Fishponds Road in 1938, the Queen Street baths were converted into a reservoir.

161.   In March 1911 Messrs. Blake of Bedford opened the Picturedrome cinema in Ickleford Road, much to the delight of the town. Programmes were shown 'at popular prices, twice nightly' to packed houses. On the opening night the audience was treated to a series of short films with titles like 'The making of a cricket bat', 'Fox Hunting', 'His mother's thanksgiving', and 'Bobby as a Bootblack'. The cinema proved so successful that it was not long before the owners made considerable improvements, including the building of a stage. Theatrical performances and boxing matches were later to become a regular feature.

162. In 1913, two years after the opening of Blake's Picturedrome, another picture palace opened its doors for the first time in Hitchin. The Playhouse had seating for over 800 people and was declared by a local paper to be 'the most artistically furnished cinema in Hertfordshire'. The auditorium, built by Newton's behind the west side of the Market Place was reached by a corridor next door to Hobley's Restaurant.

163. The Hitchin Thespians in a lavish production of *Chu Chin Chow* in 1949. In 1903, at a meeting in the Reverend G. B. Gainsford's house in Veralum Road, a decision was taken to form the Hitchin Light Operatic Society, later the Thespians. With the exception of the war years they have never failed to stage at least one production a year, often reaching very high standards. Their repertoire has covered ground from Gilbert and Sullivan to Rodgers and Hammerstein and in recent years they have given concerts of music by Brahms, Elgar and Carl Orff.

64. *A Midsummer Night's Dream*, 1951: the Bancroft Players in their first production at the Woodside open-air theatre. The theatre was formed from an old sand pit in the Dell, close to the Woodside car park. A multitude of problems beset these early productions, not least the difficulties encountered with gnats and the noise of rooks returning to roost in the trees during the evening performances. Some members of the cast kept the gnats at bay by drenching themselves with lavender water. The Dell was abandoned for many years, but recently with the building of the Queen Mother theatre nearby, organisation has become much easier and it has been successfully revived.

65. During the Second World War an entertainments society, formed to help keep up morale among townspeople and evacuees, put on a series of amateur dramatic productions. In 1945, the war over and its services no longer required, the society was disbanded and its assets made over to St Bridget's Home in Radcliffe Road. A month later, however, members re-established themselves as an amateur theatrical group that became the Bancroft Players. In this photograph they are seen in *Pygmalion*, their first production in the Town Hall in 1945.

166. People gathering for the procession to celebrate the coronation of Edward VII on 9 August 1902. The celebrations had been organised for 26 June but were postponed following the announcement that the King was seriously ill. Three hundred old people were fed in the town hall and 2,750 children were given tea as originally planned, but the procession did not take place till the coronation six weeks later. No expense was spared for the decoration of streets on the processional route. Barclays Bank is lit with electric lights, a considerable novelty at the time. The gas lamps of Cash and Co., bootmakers, can be seen on the left of the picture.

167.   Patriotism was riding high in the years before the First World War. The celebrations for the coronation of George V were even more lavish than those of his predecessor. Avenues of Venetian masts lined Sun Street, Market Place and Bancroft, each garlanded and festooned and bearing a shield representing one of the colonies. As a Royal Manor Hitchin found particular reason to celebrate the monarchy and staged a procession of the kings and queens of England. The Conservative Working Mens Club here represented the landing of the Normans on British soil with a boat specially built by P. H. Barker's, the timber merchants.

168. After the coronation procession the town's 3,000 schoolchildren were marched into the square four abreast. The children were given the following instructions: 'At the First Bugle Call – Children will come to 'attention', facing the centre of the Square and the boys will raise their caps. (Helpers behind Children). The Royal Salute will be played by the Bugles and Drums and three cheers given for the king'. This photograph appeared in the souvenir brochure and is curious in that it has been doctored to remove the lantern cupola from the Corn Exchange.

169. At approximately 11.00 a.m. the procession made its way to Butts Close where the president of the Coronation Celebrations, F. A. Delmé Radcliffe of the Priory, and the 'G' Company of the Herts Territorial Army saluted the Flag.

170. The Hertfordshire Hunt met regularly in the Market Place once a year on Boxing Day until the early 1950s, and attracted large crowds of excited onlookers. With changes in public attitudes it is unlikely that they would receive the same unmixed reception today. In this 1951 photograph a huntsman is galloping down Bucklersbury followed by boys on foot.

171. Hospital Saturday, 3 September 1921, the first of the popular parades to raise money for the North Herts. and South Beds. hospital and for the Herts. Convalescent home at St Leonards. On this occasion the parade raised a total of £242 8s. 5d. This sum was increased by a concert of the Hitchin Band in the Market Place the following day. The letters carried by women from Letchworth Spirella Factory spell out: 'PLEASE BE GENEROUS, GIVE FREELY' – as long as their bearers keep in step.

172. A local celebration. Mr. Stan Sadler, his family and neighbours, celebrating V.E. Day in Bedford Road.

173. The Priory forms the background for Hitchin's 1951 extravaganza, an historical pageant recreating 2,000 years of the town's history. Over 1,000 people took part in all; not only from Hitchin but from many of the neighbouring parishes as well. British Rail was approached and asked to offer cut-price tickets to the town for the occasion within a 35-mile radius (calculated to include London). Arranged as part of the Festival of Britain celebrations it was Hitchin's expression of relief after the constraints of the war years, but habits of austerity die hard and despite enthusiasm there was constant heartsearching about the cost of it all.

174. A scene from the 1951 Hitchin pageant in the Priory grounds: townspeople re-enact Carmelite monks signing over the original Priory to King Henry VIII at the time of the dissolution of the monasteries.

175. Her Majesty the Queen, whose childhood was largely spent at St Paul's Waldenbury near Hitchin, has many associations with the town. She attended dancing lessons with her brother at the *Sun Hotel* and was driven to school at 'Lopside', a house in Dacre Road, in a governess cart. Here she greets Isobel Harkness, the Festival Maid of Hitchin's 1951 pageant.

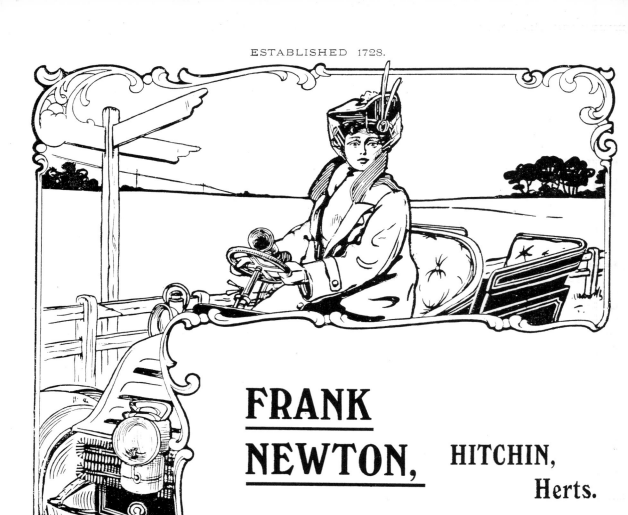